M000305368

# CheeseDosa

---

## *The Legend-Dairy Tales of a Suburban Dork*

**ADITYA SURENDRAN**

CheeseDosa Publishing

ISBN/SKU: 978-0-578-87363-3 (Hardcover)
EISBN: 978-0-578-87364-0 (e-Book)

Library of Congress Control Number: 2021914828

Portions of this book are works of fiction. Any references or resemblance to historical events, real places, or real people, living or dead, are used fictitiously and are entirely coincidental. Portions of this book are works of nonfiction. Certain names and identifying characteristics have been changed to respect subjects' privacy.

As an introduction to certain chapters, the author occasionally employs several pop culture images and/or quotes under, but not limited to, principles of fair use, limited excerpt, and educational purposes. These authors, singers, filmmakers, and other creatives and their works are both attributed here and clearly labeled on the pages wherein employed.

CHEESEDOSA, CHEESEDOSA PUBLISHING, the CHEESE-DOSA "C", and all original artworks are trademarks and/or registered trademarks of CheeseDosa Publishing and/or Aditya Surendran

All media, guest speaker, and marketing inquiries should be directed to thecheesedosa@gmail.com or follow the "Contact Us" directions found at cheesedosa.com

CheeseDosa Publishing
First Printing, 2021

# CHEESEDOSA

# CONTENTS

**INTRODUCTION**

v

*For My Father, Dilip.*

*Thank you for teaching me to laugh and love openly every day.*

*For My Mother, Kirti.*

*Thank you for teaching me to never look down nor look away.*

*To Vinay Sanapala,*

*You are the music-maker. You are the dreamer of dreams.*

*Thank you for making me believe my dream can come true.*

*And in no small way.*

*For My Wife, Melissa.*

*You are threaded in these pages.*

*You are laced in this ink.*

*You are my words--*


*You are everything and all my five things.*

*And Lastly, For You.*

*Somewhere in a world of chaos and selfishness and practicality, you picked up a book about a dork from Edison, NJ.*

*I'm not sure you'll ever truly know what that means to me as I sit here--sobbing away--hoping I make you proud ...*

*... or at least make you smile.*

**The Key, Cover Art (1992)**
*by Aditya Surendran (if not already made abundantly clear
2-3 times above)*

# INTRODUCTION

**T**his is not a cookbook.

If nothing else, friend, know that.

You should also know that even though 'CheeseDosa: The Book' is being marketed as my writing debut, this is not *technically* my first book.

*strap in for your first trip down memory lane*

The first book I ever wrote was in second grade--a handwritten science-fiction/fantasy adventure titled "The Key." With the help of a mysterious key etched with the words "This can open any door," our protagonist travels through various magical passageways leading him to other planets, dimensions and alternate realities.

As a story, it was okay--maybe even more than okay considering a second grader wrote it while in public school. I've certainly seen worse plots get TV deals.

However, I received a "B-" for my work. Heartbreaking but also understandable. The culprit was my "About the Author" section which took up over 75% of the book. If that's not bad enough, this ATA section meandered through my life with unnecessary details: my parents' immigrant journey to my favorite video games; from a fall I had on my bike to how much I liked my teacher, Dr. Radice. The key, the characters, and even actually completing the assignment were all an afterthought.

Looking back on it, I should probably have received a far lower grade.

My parents were not at all pleased about the B- and definitely made sure I knew this. However, the dust settled eventually. And then, for the first and only time, I saw my parents take a non-A graded paper and stick it onto the fridge. I still don't really know what compelled them to do so.

Maybe they intuited my love of storytelling.

Maybe they'd juxtaposed their childhood and rigorous Indian school system--which never would have allowed such fanciful story assignments--and realized how lucky we were to be in America.

Maybe they secretly loved that I was such a momma's boy and had dotingly written about them...

... or maybe it was something else entirely.

It meant a lot regardless.

I mention this upfront because, in many ways, "Cheese-Dosa: The Book" is just a massive 'About the Author' section that has slowly metastasized since second grade, fed with over 20 years of more memories: new loves lost, new loves found, crippling fears overcome or succumbed to, and, of course, a seemingly limitless supply of embarrassing situations.

**So welcome Welcome WELCOME to my book!**

You're going to learn about my parents, my favorite video games, so much food (even though I insist this is still NOT a cookbook), and many teachers--literally and figuratively--that have taught me so much. The stories are all true and adhere to one simple rule: the plot must be boring. But, hopefully through getting to know me, you'll care about these stories anyway.

And, if you're anything like me, you're a little boring sometimes or a little dorky more than sometimes. So maybe you'll see some of yourself in these stories too.

Truly, nothing would make me happier.

Should we begin on such a cute and sensitive note?

Um. No, thank you! Eesh.

## Unnecessary Technical Details About the Book

You should also know that this is an entirely self-published book in every way imaginable. A local artist, Sarah McVane, realized my vision of the cover, an actual scene from my childhood. My wife Melissa illustrated many of the in-book drawings. And yours truly wrote the stories, tested them in live open mic settings, edited them (poorly), and ultimately entered them into this unwieldy program sponsored by Ingram Publishing in order to bring this final book to you.

Long story long, this is an organic, grass-to-mouth book with all the speckled imperfection of a farm-raised robin's egg. And if all you can think about now is "why are we doing a farm analogy?" or "do robin farms exist?" then there's a lot of disappointment awaiting you over the next 23 chapters.

But there might also be some laughs.

So, that's all. Enjoy the show!

\* \* \*

Oh wait. You'll need something before you begin your journey. It opens all of the chapters to follow and is my most precious belonging.

It's a single, golden, magical key.

Please handle it with care, even if it doesn't work right every time or takes you somewhere you didn't want to go ... or disappoints you in some way. Just know it means well-- even if it spends a little too much time talking about itself.

Love you all.

Looking forward to our time together.

*Plays 1990s United Center
Jordan Era Intro Music

STANDING, AT 8.5 INCHES TALL...

FROM BOMBAY, INDIA...

BY WAY OF EDISON, NJ...

**Aditya**

---

**Adi**

---

**Jay**

---

**AC**

---

**'Ya**

---

**Dhoti-Pants**

---

**A-tit-ya**

---

**Dorkasaur**

---

**MUNFAG**

---

**Parents Bane**

---

**Thorn of Melissa**

---

**Destroyer of Lil Wayne Karaoke**

---

**The Longwinded Braggart**

---

**Kumbalathparambil Surendran**

---

**Presents**

---

CHEESEDOSA: THE BOOK

PART ONE

"Look. Our family just doesn't have the genetics. Maybe if there was a ping pong team. Could you start a ping pong team?"

**Dilip Surendran**

*Reflections On a Son's Basketball Team Tryouts* (1996)

# | one |

# My Plenty of Fish

**Edison, NJ (1992)**

The first time--and only time--I've been fishing I was eight years old.

My dad and I head out to a lake near our place—Roosevelt Park for those of you who might know it.

Mom reads a trashy novel by the water and lets us have our fantasy where we bring home meat like impressive providers, catching something with our bare hands to give to the female who will cook it.

We have glorious goals of eating dinner from our catch, but a few hours in, dad and I begin to realize fishing takes a basic amount of skill.

And we do not have that.

However, this skill seems to be within the grasp of a Chinese grandfather near us and a white father and son on the other side of the lake. The grandfather owns two buckets, one for the fish he is catching and the other for his live bait. I can't really see what kind of bait the duo has across the lake but the dad dons a floppy taupe fishing hat with bait stuck to it.

Our bait, however, was purchased at "The Rag Shop," an arts and crafts store with no official fishing aisle per se.

Note to reader: The Rag Shop would file for Chapter 7 bankruptcy ten years later. The foldup sent shockwaves through the fifth grade diorama community. Two amateur anglers also have yet to make a full recovery.

"Son, get the bait."

I look down at my hands. Our bait is a red and white plastic ball with colorful neon feathers haphazardly stuck all over it.

I begin to realize, as our hopes are cast out onto the lake, that our fate rests upon the whims of a plastic and pregnant clownlike ball. And refusing to even sink below the water, luring fish seems to be an act far too pedestrian for the buoyed diva.

the real one looked even stupider than this one

Hours pass and no fish. I sigh.

Our national pride--only 4 years in the US at the time--and our apparent inability to naturally provide food for our family--something even sparrows can do--begin to eat away at us.

That's when we see a dead fish floating near the lake's shore. We poke this yellowish flounder with a stick. It looks nothing like the one from The Little Mermaid. And it is definitely dead.

My dad and I look at each other.

We think about our journey to America and how this fishing trip represents a dream that our relatives back home would never do–at least not the wealthy ones. We look across the lake and find the white father and his son bonding over their fishing successes.

We think of how mom will look at our empty-handed hands and say something droll like "did you two have fun on your fishing … experiment?" emphasizing and drawing out the last word as long as she can, then returning to her torrid romance novel.

We look to our right and see the old Chinese man catch yet another fish.

It becomes clear what we have to do.

We grab the biggest stick we can find and begin to drag the dead fish to the shore. Our talented counterparts watch with horror as we lead the dead fish with our stick and roll it onto a newspaper.

"We got one!" dad and I scream. We jump around--arms and legs akimbo--radiating joy.

And, looking back on it now, we did get one.

For males.

For India.

For dad.

For me.

**Will**: You missed Pudge Fisk's home run to have a drink with a woman you had never met?

**Sean:** I just slid my ticket across the table and said "sorry fellas, I gotta go see about a girl."

**Good Will Hunting (1997)**

# | two |

# My Good Meal Hunting

### Childhood (1984-2002)

As a young kid, it was not fun being good at math while also being poor.

A classroom lesson in division or fractions could easily trigger a dinner memory from the day before — which might've been a single Nathan's hot dog ... served family style.

And if I ever felt blue about being a few cents short on lunch money, both decimals and scientific notation would put their arms around me and say:

*"Don't worry. It gets smaller."*

This might've been a simple Pe^rt problem for our family. Take some **P**rincipal, compound **e** by the **R**ate of interest, and then just wait for **T**–time–to come and rescue us.

You know. Save money, basically.

However, with no actual money to save, our Pert problems were Pert shampoo problems. On any given Monday, I'd have to ask myself "was this the week mom adds water to the shampoo to extend its life?"

\* \* \*

We don't have these problems anymore. But I dredge this all up now because five minutes ago my wife just said "yes" to something big.

### Rahway, NJ (2020)

"You're sure, right?" I ask, taking out my phone slowly.

"Yea, I mean, I'm obviously a little nervous. But it's been really boring these past 2 months of covid-19. And you've been great. Let's just try it."

My heart starts to race.

I'm paranoid, but slowly slide my finger across the phone to unlock it.

*"This isn't a trick, right?"*

*"No."*

*"I just want to come clean, Mel. I used to do this while you were away on work trips to China. You're sure it's ok?"*

*"Oh I already knew about that. I'd see it on your credit card statement, clear as day."*

I scroll through my screen, page after page, until I find it. There, looking as patriotic as ever, is the Domino's Pizza App.

2 pizzas, two toppings, $5.99 each. Seems simple enough, right? Wrong.

I take a deep breath. Time seems to slow down.

I get to work.

The app let's you choose some other options for $5.99 instead of a pizza. Bread twists, 8 cubes of chicken, a salad that reminds you God probably doesn't exist, and a bunch of other options with embarrassingly low CPD.

CPD, as we all know--even though I'm making it up right now--is Calories Per Dollar. And, once you harness that metric, choosing pizza is not only the correct choice, but the only choice.

So I skip past those inferior options, click on the scaffolding of the first pizza and fall into a deep meditative state.

"Oo, thin crust could be fun," cuts through the silence.

A far cry. A voice that sounds like Melissa's seems to reach from the beyond with deeply inefficient thoughts, seemingly oblivious to CPD.

I upgrade the pizza to 'deep dish,' which I know will cost nothing.

I'm confident because this particular Domino's is run by technologically illiterate but extremely attentive Egyptians, traits which make for this free upgrade and all other kinds of arbitrage throughout an order.

No changes for the sauce. That will come later. And so comes the time for toppings.

Because the app let's you divide the pizza into two sides, I place pepperoni and olives on one side of Pizza #1 and onions and a meat topping called "Philly Cheesesteak" on the other.

Adding cheddar cheese to this side would have made an actual philly cheesesteak sitting atop my pizza, but then they win. Just one extra topping on one half is enough to raise the price by what could've been almost another pizza.

For Pizza #2, Mel's pizza, I should probably introduce another metric to you, CTD. As she's vegetarian, the difference in CPD, calories per dollar, is negligible—*how many more calories can you get from a diced tomato versus spinach after all?*

And, so, since the toppings are already free, I instead look to CTD, Cost to Domino's. What's the biggest dent I can make in their empire?

This means olives and mushrooms on one side and convincing Melissa that jalapenos and pineapple go together for the other.

After I put the order in, I call Domino's. Ali picks up.

I ingratiate myself to him, explaining these smartphones are too smart for me—that I made a big mistake and wanted to order three pizzas, not two. This add-on could have been done on the app, but ordering the third pizza this way gets me 20 rewards points instead of just 10, doubling my speed to another free pizza someday.

"Also, Ali, can I be honest with you?"

He replies with something or another.

"This one time I ordered from you, there was no tomato sauce on my pizza. I don't think it was Yasmine—she's always been great. But could you make sure there's sauce?"

*You should know I am being honest, even though "that one time" was nearly three years ago almost to the date.*

"Of course, actually, sir, is extra sauce ok for you?"

"You're too kind, Ali. Shukran."

I can almost hear this teenager smiling. So I know it's time to go for it.

"Hey, one last thing, this is going to sound stupid, but I thought the cheesesteak topping came with cheese."

I savor the pause.

3.

2.

1.

Three seconds should be enough.

"You think you could throw on cheddar cheese on that side too?"

\* \* \*

I open up the Domino's app to track this pizza. Ali has processed the order and Yasmine places the toppings. Step three is the oven getting "fired up" and ready. Ahmed boxes it and the pizza is off for delivery.

It's all so efficient. The visual charts look so clean.

But I imagine behind all that is a family. Growing up. Hustling.

The same as me.

But I remind myself that at least a pizza is easier to divide than a hot dog.

\* \* \*

So, that brings us to right now. Melissa takes a bite of the pizza. I await her praise.

"You know it's obviously not as good as Il Forno, but this isn't bad!"

"Isn't bad," I smile.

I suppose she doesn't need to know how an entire cathedral, a Taj Mahal, has been built in her honor inside that cardboard box.

She had invoked Il Forno a Legna, our local pizza shop that only used the freshest and most traditional of ingredients. They also allege their forno a legna–or wood-burning furnace–had been shipped from Naples. How a brave little forno made its way across the world and why it decided to rest indefinitely in Rahway, New Jersey is beyond me.

I begin to bite into my Philly Cheesesteak frankenpizza, the pinnacle of CPD…

"I know these flavors remind you of your childhood, so we can enjoy it from time to time. Especially during covid."

My brow furrows as I attempt to digest both my wife's words and the low-grade meat, paper thin onions, bright yellow cheddar, and "real" mozzarella cheese, a term Domino's lobbied for so that "real" could mean whatever they wanted.

I don't think I'd ever actually cared about the flavors at all. And suddenly, I feel this strange feeling with each bite my wife took of her pizza.

> *What is the point in her having to eat this?*
> *Is this what guilt feels like?*
> *This certainly doesn't feel like a win.*

The next week I insist we order from Il Forno.

Mel surveys the menu and wants to share a $20 pizza and a $12 burrata salad. I am not at all excited about this healthy and pricey excursion.

But then I look at the menu. There, on completely different sides of the menu, lay a $5 side salad and a $15 burrata pizza.

*By now, are you thinking what I'm thinking?*

Maybe there's a way to make this work.

"When the world is itself draped in the mantle of night, the mirror of the mind is like the sky in which thoughts twinkle like stars."

**KHUSHWANT SINGH**
**DELHI: A NOVEL (1990)**

- Ever wonder what those sparkly dots are up there? ... I always thought they were balls of gas burning billions of miles away.

- Pumbaa, with you, everything's gas.

**THE LION KING (1994)**

# | three |

## My Space Race

When I was a child, I wanted to go to space.

My ceiling had thousands of the tiniest glow in the dark stickers. Once laboriously applied, they represented all the stars and named constellations. The northern hemisphere laid above my pillow and the southern hemisphere was splayed out above the foot of my bed.

But on the long march to becoming 30, star stuff gave way to the stuff of life. Some awful, some awe-inspiring, but all did their part to blot out the sky.

And yet, a few weeks before my 30th birthday, something arrives.

**From: Jiten Dave**
**Wednesday, 3:07pm**
**May 21st, 2013**

*Hey Cousin,*

*Greetings from sunny Los Angeles. Just wanted to share some good news. Our son, Rohan, reached the national finals of a middle school patch design contest sponsored by NASA.*

*The winner's patch will be sewn into the suit of an astronaut traveling into space at the next launch. Voting ends on Saturday morning, so please try to vote if you can.*

*Love, Jiten*

A link to a SurveyMonkey site follows.

I stare at the screen blankly for minutes.

Then twitch.

Maybe I won't get to the stars, and maybe neither will my nephew, but this patch – this piece of cloth stitched with my dream – maybe it can get to space.

I'm at work and dramatically explain to my coworkers why this matters. It is a team that grows moustaches for Movember every year, so this is an easy sell. The idea catches fire and forty votes are docked within the hour.

In the evening, I look at the online scoreboard for the first time. The four patch finalists are laid out before me. Votes are 2, 11, 20, 52.

We are well in the lead with a girl or boy named Xie Wang in second. I feel confident about Rohan's patch and even kind of bad for the one with two votes.

*Dillon's is a patch that, evidently, only a mother could love.*

I get into bed and try voting on my phone. It is the second time that day, but it works.

*Interesting.*

I try again and receive the prompt informing me I have already voted.

*Weird.*

My eyes grow heavy as I look out of my window at the sky. "See you soon," I eke out, half-dreaming.

"Two more days till the stars."

The next day the whole family gets involved. Mom and dad's coworkers, my other cousin's third graders, a few strangers from the Metropark train station, anyone who will listen to our story are logging in votes.

When I get home from work, the scoreboard shows lots of movement, well mostly. Dillon only managed to get a third vote, probably just his dad, but the rest of us are off to the races:

3, 25, 67, 102.

We are still in front and, in fact, have increased our lead.

But something about the score of 67 feels unsettling, makes me feel unsafe.

*Did Xie really triple his or her score in a day?*

I get out my phone and try voting again.

103.

On a hunch, I completely turn off my phone, turn it on again and try voting.

104.

I'll spare you exact details of what follows, but when I call my cousin immediately thereafter, words like cached memory, IP addresses, hard resets, and a bunch of other jibberish lead us to a simple conclusion:

This vote can be rigged.

We both vote in tandem for about 2 hours until we reach 401--since we're apparently criminal masterminds now, we don't want a round number to arouse suspicion. We then call it a night.

Friday morning is the final full day of voting and I half-expect to see some kind of mercy rule applied; these are kids after all.

I check the numbers to see if they have declared us the winner early, but I see something else entirely.

3, 26, 401 ... 503.

Somehow Xie had overtaken us while we were sleeping. Well, not "somehow," we all know exactly how. Now, every time I refresh the page, Xie's votes keep jumping higher. 504, 506, 511.

My face goes hot.

I frantically start voting but can't keep pace—for each vote I dock there are 2 or 3 more votes going to Xie. I give up when I reach 500. Xie is already at 750 and the votes climb throughout the afternoon until reaching 1,000. There, it hovers at twice our score, taunting me.

I am shattered.

Hopeless. Helpless.

But then the phone rings. Jiten, Rohan's dad, has come up with a plan.

We play dead for the whole day and gather online as a family at 10pm. Eight of us across 4 cities. We are dialed into Ramesh Uncle's work conference line to communicate; but no one is speaking.

Nothing needs to be said.

9:58, 9:59; 10pm.

The clicking rumbles across the conference line.

With Firefox, Chrome, and Internet Explorer open on each of our computers; and iPhones, Samsung phones, Note Tablets, and iPads flanking, we are an interconnected Indian-American mission control seemingly with enough technology to send an actual rocket into space.

45 minutes is all it takes to approach 1,000, but now Xie and many other Wangs are back on the site.

Both patch tallies are rising at a feverish pace.

This continues for hours but, around 1am, some of our east coast family–and a few Wangs–start to drop out.

At 3am, Jiten and Rohan say they are going to sleep.

That leaves just me and Xie.

I am out ahead by about 250 votes and Xie has slowed down to about 1-2 votes a minute, an easy clip to keep ahead of.

At 4:30am, Xie stops entirely.

I don't.

I am ready to go to infinity and beyond.

In the absolute dark of my room, the pale light of four screens make me feel like I am floating through complete deep space. Eventually, the sunrise breaks me out of my spell and by the 8am closing time, the scores are locked in.

Dillon has 4.

I'd felt a kinship with him during those lonely hours and ended up giving Dillon my final vote.

Then 32, 3,047, and 12,555.

\* \* \*

Rohan, Xie Wang and their parents are called to the principal's office later that day and an impassioned, quasi-legal argument ensues about whether this was cheating or not.

I haven't given that question much shrift.

What I do know is we were trying to get to space, trying to claim something that has always been out of reach. And maybe dreams don't come true exactly as planned, but aim high, keep your loved ones close, and get there. Get there however you can.

Rohan's patch returned to Earth a year later. Its voyage reminds me that we came from the stars.

And, perhaps, more importantly ...

that we are not alone.

**The Patch We Voted On**

**The Patch That Flew**
*(NASA, in good conscience, felt
improvements were needed)*

I cried because I had no shoes until I met a man who had no feet.

~ *Kirti Surendran*
*... quoting Helen Keller*

*...anytime I wanted new sneakers.*

# | four |

## My Shoes

**Edison, New Jersey (December 2016)**

*Our shoes decide what kind of person we are going to be.*

Here I stand directly in front of this phrase, contemplating its meaning. It is printed in a flourishing script worthy of a constitution or declaration of rights.

It's the kind of quote that makes you think. It's the kind of quote that might have been uttered by Gandhi or Mother Theresa during a long march.

*Our shoes decide what kind of person we are going to be.*

As I stand where I stand, though, I feel a strange feeling. Because as I stand where I stand, I realize I am standing in a line.

At a DSW.

I am one bead amongst a lengthy string getting or returning shoes at a shoe store. The day after Christmas.

"Our shoes decide what kind of person we are going to be" is the slogan in the line area emblazoned across all the lamps lifted beside the not-so-golden exit door.

The forty-something lady in front of me is buying Under Armour crossfit sneakers. I imagine her shoes will soon decide her to be someone ready to make aggressive changes, be more direct, ask for what she wants in life. And protect her house.

She is scolding her teenage daughter who is buying Uggs … boots which I can only imagine must be for a self-actualizing trip to the Arctic or adjacent tundra. Definitely not to shuttle from her dorm to class and back again.

Me? I'm no different. I am buying these. All red Nikes.

The person I am going to be is someone who clearly will

require a lot of attention. As I consider the purchase, a voice inside my head whispers, "Just do it."

As I sit in that immovable line, a war of words between mother and daughter erupts— "Why do you need those Uggs to be warm if you're going to wear them with booty shorts?" the mom asks aggressively, directly, and, remarkably, without her Under Armour crossfits even on yet.

I look at the quote one last time.

Like me, you think you see the quote for what it is. Some meaningless phrase there to just sell shoes. But we're about to travel through time and space, a full eternity of 2 days from now and a cosmic, well, 1.7 miles from this DSW, to learn one thing: we can be wrong.

"Our shoes decide what kind of person we are going to be." By the end of this story, I submit to you that they can.

*Metropark, 2 days later.*

Metropark is a major train hub in New Jersey, ferrying tens of thousands of Edison commuters into New York City every day. Of those tens of thousands, approximately tens of thousands of them are also South Asian.

Day in. Day out.

This means that you, someone you know, or someone going to a desi wedding will come through its hallowed walls tired, hungry, and yearning to have dosa. And that's where I am right now in this story, in a line. Again.

This time a bead amongst a scattering of many more waiting for a train.

**Cricket ads and other desi paraphernalia riddle Metropark Station**

"Great shoes, bro" I hear a younger version of myself say. He looks like he is in college and it looks like he and his girlfriend are off to their respective internships.

"It's no big deal," I lie in response. "They're just shoes. These are great for the gym, though" I lie again.

2017 is in two more days.  I'll resolve to actually go to the gym then.

The train arrives and I stop smiling at my younger self.  I finagle my way through the crowd to get on first, passing the young, old, and infirm.

There's rowdiness, shoving, a general acceptance that you must leave your humanity on the platform if you intend to get onto this train. I manage to put one shoe onto the train entrance and proceed to put the second one on.

Suddenly, I feel a scraping from my calf all the way down my leg. My shoe dislodges and starts to dangle on my toes.

For one brilliant Schroedinger moment, I am neither wearing nor not wearing this shoe. But then the unthinkable happens.  My shoe falls off my foot.

But it does not land in the train or on the platform. It dives right through the middle and lands on the tracks. Ten feet down. Looking like a bloodied forest animal.

My rage begins to build.  I turn around to see the culprit. It doesn't matter that he is an old man. He looks embarrassed but shoves past me to get on the train as do all the other passengers.

What follows is fueled by the wrath of a thousand lines

I've been in and will be in. It is fueled by that perceived indifference. And, if I'm being honest, probably fueled by a presidential election and the fact that he is an old white man in a suit that doesn't care that there's a shoe on the track.

"My shoe is on the track," I shout. "My shoe is on the track and you don't care." It starts like a nursery rhyme if not for my red face and spittle coming out of my mouth. "You don't care because you're in such a big rush. Right, Mr. God Damn Important?"

He leaves nonchalantly and behind him is the younger me with his girlfriend. They look at me with horror. I hobble off the train refusing to take off the other sneaker for symmetry.

I can't walk back home which is twenty minutes and presumably longer with one shoe. Getting on the train and walking over 40 minutes through Manhattan doesn't seem like an option either.

I realize that I don't have any place to go and no place to return to. This, in a way, makes me homeless. I time out how long it is till the next train and decide when and where I can jump down onto the tracks. As I'm weighing the pros and cons of this potential suicide, the conductor comes out.

"Should I even ask how this happened?" I think about drowning that careless old man with my words. Ending his polished image with a tale of high crime and intrigue.

But then I see the conductor smiling. He's the only one smiling for miles during such a morning commute. He chuckles and pops the floor of the train entrance.

"Wow!" I shout as I'd never seen that happen.

He goes down some steps until he is at track level and bellows from below "could you please describe the shoe for me?"

I start belly laughing. "It's red. Pretty much looks like this one," as I dangle my left foot over the tracks so he can see it.

He smiles at me and I smile back.

I get on the train with my shoes reunited and see my younger self.

"Holy shit, bro. How did you get it back?" he says as his girlfriend and about three onlookers also want to know.

"Well, let me tell you," I sit down across the aisle from him so I'm properly staged for everyone to see and hear my story.

"Shhhhh!!!!!"

A cruel twist.

I'm told by other passengers that I'm in the quiet car where absolutely no talking is allowed.

But I smile. My shoes had decided that I didn't need the attention anymore. And even if I'd never get a chance to tell this story after all -- that's okay.

**Mr. Feeny:**  Believe in yourselves. Dream. Try. Do good.

**Topanga:**  Don't you mean "do well?"

**Mr. Feeny:**  No, I mean ... do good.

**Boy Meets World, Final Scene**
May 5th, 2000

# | five |

# My Nicks and Scratches

**Woodrow Wilson Middle School Playground**

**Edison, NJ ( 1997)**

To be the biggest nerd in middle school sucks. To be the second biggest one is better. But only mildly.   Trust me. I know.

Your only true friend is the biggest nerd, but your greatest fear is being supplanted by him, of becoming him.

Prakash.

Prakash is Indian, slightly portly, and constantly turns phrases into perverted jokes in order to gain acceptance. Basically me.

But he has a British accent, so as far as I'm concerned, we have nothing in common.

Yet, in the mornings, the playground is where we divide up like various species at a watering hole in the Serengeti. And Prakash and I are often inseparable; playing catch with stuff we find on the ground, currently a dirty tennis ball that the far cooler children had determined no longer useful for wall ball.

Just like our friendship, we start friendly, lobbing whatever projectile we find in a lazy arc, smiling as the other displays a nominal amount of athleticism in catching it. Though our angst and general boyhood always force our hand as we progressively speed up our throws.

Inexorably, we wind up whipping whatever we have at the other and shattering whatever flimsy rules comprise this loose game.

Nerds 3-5 are considering joining us somewhere in the middle of this buildup when Prakash goes into full whip mode way too early with the dirty tennis ball. The hurl lands a direct hit to my crotch area of my Osh Kosh B'Gosh chinos.

I can feel my grip loosening over my Nerd #2 status as Nerds 3-5 begin to laugh maniacally. The ignominy of running down the tennis ball and continuing the game is too great. I try to find something that will hurt.

Even in my anger, I know a rock is excessive and will carry with it serious punishment. A pine cone won't fly nearly as fast as needed and, when hitting Prakash's forgiving body, will bounce off impotently. I keep hunting until I find it.

There it is. Pure.

Its aerodynamics carved over eons of evolution. Simple.

To explain, we have to take a departure, traveling to a WordPress blog I found about trees titled "The Most Dangerous Tree in the Suburbs:"

> There was a time not too long ago when the Sweet Gum Tree was a popular choice for suburban yards. It grows relatively fast, has a pleasing symmetrical shape and fabulous fall color . . . In 2012, the Arbor Day Foundation gave out thousands of young Sweet Gum saplings to the children of Springfield, Illinois who eagerly planted them along the sidewalks in front of their homes.

*Who has the time and will to chronicle all this? I scroll to the next page ...*

But today, the Sweet Gum has [all but] disappeared. The Sweet Gum's primary liability, according to the Lazy Landscaper–*yes, a real publication*–are the thousands of spiny brown seed balls–gum balls if you will–that it casts upon the ground around it.

These "hard, brown, spiky balls can create some serious hazards. Not only can they wound you if you slip and fall onto them, they can also roll unexpectedly, causing sprained ankles. And don't try to run your lawnmower over them, as when airborne they are as dangerous as grenades."

As dangerous as grenades.

There, at my feet on the playground, is a spiky gum ball for my taking. I lift it up and clutch it in my hand, evaluating its weight and dimensions.

I look up at Prakash and the other three nerds. Like a quarterback, pitcher, or Ryu from Street Fighter, I build up a furious amount of potential energy and then unleash.

The spiky ball races out faster than anything I've ever seen. So fast that, within milliseconds, I lose the ability to trace its whereabouts. A few seconds pass by and I see all four nerds looking shocked. Then I hear three clear words cut through the din of the playground.

"What. The. Fuck."

A tiny pathway opens up and it becomes clear the words came from Nick.

In my anger, I had hit Nick. The Hick.

He is massaging his mullet and staring directly at me. With the swagger of a horror movie villain, he begins walking firmly as I process what just happened.

*Okay, Adi, you just hit Nick the hick. He's bigger, stronger, and faster than you. He also has been in at least five fights this week. This far outstrips your zero of all time. You need to diffuse this situation. Offer your lunch money. Wait you don't have lunch money, just some of mom's leftover Gujurati food. No, that will only make him madder. Grovel. Grovel like a fool.*

"I can't believe that happened, man. Dude. I had no idea–"

He is getting far too close now with no sign of stopping. The crowd around us looks delirious—they won't accept it ending in a pleasant handshake and a laugh about how sweet gumballs travel way more erratically than one anticipates.

It's too much attention. We're going to get into trouble at this rate. All kinds of obscenities are erupting from Nick. Some of them I hadn't even learnt yet. I can't handle the pressure.

"Shhh, just shut up. Just shut up!" I plead with him. I don't want to get into trouble, but it's too late now. This is happening. We lock horns. The fight begins.

I hold one of his arms. As he uses the other to swing at me, I begin rotating out of his way. This continues three times, four times. And I realize I'm not getting hit, though a little dizzy with all the spinning.

"Gross. Why the hell are you dancing?" is the last thing I hear from a crowd growing very tired of this samba as a couple of hall monitors break up the fight.

Trig, French, and a bunch of other classes I normally delight in now feel like a completely different experience.

"Heard you fought Nick the Hick?" says a girl from my honors classes. Days would pass before I process that an actual girl spoke to me. In the moment, though, all I can think about is what's going to happen next.

And then it happens.

"Um, Adi-Taya Surenno-nodon" blares the intercom as if my family lineage could be traced back to the Jurassic period, "please report to the principal's office."

Nick is already in the room as I walk in trembling. He looks comfortable, in his element. He's been here before.

The principal asks me to take a seat.

"How about one of you tells me what happened today morning?"

I look pathetic and terrified. I'm thinking of a way to craft this story in a way that still ensures I will go to Harvard or something similar six years from now. The promise of a good college was supposed to be the consolation prize for serving all these years in solitary nerditude -- even unironically using SAT Verbal section words like "ignominy" and "inexorable" in casual conversations.

I realize that no amount of smarts will help me keep this off my file. I start to shiver. The principal looks at me confused and takes out a tissue box he didn't expect he'd need for a fight between two teenage boys.

I am about to begin when Nick launches—

"I'm just minding my business, right? Bam! I get hit in the head with this pine cone thing. I turn around and I see this kid looking at me. I walk up to him, right? He doesn't apologize at all. I say, 'dude what the fuck' — sorry Mr. Andrews — I say 'why did you hit me?' And then this kid just starts telling me to shut up. Over and over again. Shut up. Just shut up. We were in each other's faces, so we fought."

As I go over his story, I realize that nothing he is saying is a lie. Well, other than the fact that it wasn't a pine cone. I break down crying and grab 1, 2, 3 tissues consecutively.

Harvard is gone.

"I'm supposed to believe that load of horseshit? Someone hit you with a pine cone and so you beat up this nerd?" The principal says as I look up with tears and hope in my eyes.

"You're getting the usual, Nick. Now both of you out of my office."

We both step out of the room and I think I've made an enemy for life. I immediately look at Nick once we're in the hall.

"Hey, I'm sorry. So sorry. And I'm sorry that I didn't apologize before."

He gives me a look as if a fly was buzzing near his ear. "Dude. Who cares? But why did you cry?"

I would find out that the usual for Nick was 3 days of detention. He was expelled before the end of the year. He didn't seem to care about the injustice of it all. Meanwhile, I nicked Nick but got away unscathed.

\* \* \*

It was a strange feeling back then, realizing that being a nerd has its privileges. It's a strange feeling now. I see it everywhere. Staying quiet here. A little lie there. A bit of obscure data analysis explaining why this department needs layoffs. Hiding behind an algorithm to justify why those families no longer have a 401k.

Over the last few years, there's been a lot of people like Nick that seem at odds with those like us, lots of hurtful words being hurled back and forth. And the gap between us seems to be getting larger every day. There's no answer. At least, none that I've found.

And, yet, an inescapable fact gnaws at me. That sweet gumball was a seed, and I used it as a weapon. This set into motion everything else.

So if there's one thing I've learned from the playground that day, it's that I can be the most dangerous tree in the suburb, but I'd rather tell stories and make things grow.

- **This is about $100. Are you sure?**

- **Yes, Mom. \*Wipes away tears\***

- **Ok. I'm just saying, we can get 10 more of them at this same price.**

- Kirti considers complex tail
surgery for her son's gerbil.
*Edison, NJ (1996)*

*Surgery is successful.*

*Two weeks later, Jabbu eats his own poop.*

*Commits suicide.*

# | six |

# My Shelter

'Twas in another lifetime,
one of toil and blood
When blackness was a virtue
the road was full of mud
He came in from the wilderness,
a creature void of form
Come in, I said, I'll give ya
Shelter from the storm

**Bob Dylan (1975)**

### Edison, NJ (2020)

When I married my wife, who is irrefutably Caucasian, I knew two things would happen.

First, I would need to learn—and at least pretend to care—about artists like Bob Dylan.

And, second, I knew the day would come when we had to have a very particular discussion. And that day was today.

So I had my list prepared.

"Melissa, these are four reasons we should NOT get a dog:

    1. I work in the city and you travel every other week, it would not be fair to the dog

*You see, you put the argument that shows you're a compassionate human being first.*

    2. If we're thinking about kids, why rush into even more responsibility

*Then, you make a point that is only loosely connected to create fear and confusion.*

    3. We have so many friends who have dogs, they're always complaining.

*Next, you throw your friends under the bus. It's not like they're in the room, so no harm done.*

4. We can become Wag walkers and get paid to hang out with dogs over the weekend

*Least effective, but as a semi-Gujurati, I was particularly proud of the last point.*

* * *

For two years, this plan worked or at least kept the peace. When Mel's itch grew strong, we'd occasionally volunteer at this one shelter, Funny Paws.

It's run by this Trunchbull-type woman who is able to peer right into my soul. She knew everything about me and rarely offered me any of the free munchkins they'd have out at adoption events at our Petco.

"Her name is Donna," Mel says on the way back to our car. "And you don't need any munchkins."

*She's right. I should walk more.*

"Oh, by the way, Donna and I had an idea..."

I find out that the two have formed an alliance and already agreed in principle to a 2-week fostering of a beagle. All they need is my sign-off. I stutter through my typical 4 objections, but they don't seem to apply to this short-term setup. I am not prepared.

Hard to cite what would be "fair to the dog," when the alternative is the dog dying or turning into glue or whatever happens to them when they're not fostered.

And, so, I lose.

Limply, I do manage to carve out one pork barrel provision. Mel agrees to watch this one anime I'd been trying to get her to watch with me for 7 years. With us being homebound because of this dog, I figure Naruto would be a silver lining to this new, deeply provincial, domesticated life.

I was at work when it arrived a week or so later.

\* \* \*

The texts and photos come rushing in:

"He's in the car!"

"I think he's going to poop!"

*A few minutes later...*

"He hasn't pooped"

*Later came the selfies.*

"Look at him and his big, floppy ears."

"He LOVES his bed"

"You think he'll poop?"

*And this onslaught ended with:*

"He doesn't look like a Bob."

The shelter had given this batch a bunch of old white rocker names. Bruce Springsteen, Elvis Pressley, Mick Jagger–badasses basically–and our new temporary roommate had been named Bob Dylan.

I come home to find Bob, tail between his legs, hiding his face in his dog bed, which is placed inside an octagon-shaped toddler fence. So I move to the couch next to Bob's area and turn on the TV.

Mel begins to give me a recap of the day–it is strikingly familiar to the minutes I'd been getting over text.

Bob comes out of his bed and saunters over. He stares down at my feet.

"He was so scared when he was in the car. And I think

when I walked him home, it was the first time he felt grass," Mel recaps.

I reach out my hand and push his big floppy right ear back. On the inside is a tattoo "666 666."

"Yea, and we're not sure why he hasn't barked yet. I read about these medical testing dogs having their vocal chords removed," Mel continues. "But that might just be a rumor, they might just not be socialized to bark."

Bob puts his front paws on top of my knees. I look into his eyes for the first time. They feel infinitely sad.

"Hey! No!" Melissa says sternly, jolting me. Bob looks confused and unperches.

"I don't want him thinking he can hop on the couch. You have to teach them early."

Startled, he moves back to his bed, leaving Mel and I alone on the couch. I put on Naruto, excited to share everything about every moment about the first episode. About 10 minutes in, Mel leaves and goes to sleep.

A few minutes later, Bob pops out of his pack-and-play. He's been watching through the gate and now sits right beside me on the floor.

He absorbs everything about episode 1, the journey of a misunderstood kid ninja shunned by his village.

I queue up the next episode. As the same 90 second music intro begins, he tries getting back up on the couch. He seems more comfortable resting on me while standing on two legs than standing on four.

"Ok, Bob, so, this second episode is kind of filler to be honest. It's just Naruto taking on a mentee, this preschooler Konohamaru, who's this even smaller annoying kid."

He hops up on the couch. I look at him just living his life and don't have the heart to tell him to get down.

I start to play with his ears and hold up the left floppy one to the light.

*231 321*

"Bob," I think. "It's a good name."

\* \* \*

The middle of this story takes on the ramblings of a typical irritating dog lover.

Bob's first walk – he is terrified of the apartment hallway and hugs the walls the entire time. But within 3 days, he runs for the first time, and I think it might be the first time he's smiled.

*It's also the first time I've been on a walk three days in a row.*

Something about that first run brings on his first poop. It is glorious and both Melissa and I breathe a sigh of relief.

I'll spare the details and skip right to the call.

\* \* \*

It is the Trunchbull. Bob has found his forever home within a week. Taking him in is a young professional Greek mother with an adorable teenager whose Instagram account for her cat has more friends than mine.

Melissa doesn't have it in her to come give Bob away, so it falls to me.

So here I am--in this deeply mediocre Petco--looking at a bunch of idiots in their cat sweaters and dog-pun t-shirts. I guess I expect something magical to happen, but no such luck.

I have my final moments with Bob, hug him tight, and ask him to add me to his Insta. I wish there was something wise I'd said to him, but he's learned so much on his own.

I give my cellphone number to the mom, hand him off to the teen and ask her to take good care of Bob. She looks shyly at the ground and says, "we were thinking of calling him Luke."

It shouldn't matter but this takes me by surprise. I'm a little off balance.

"Of course you should call him Luke! Bob's his slave name, after all," I joke--poorly--as this kind teenager looks at me with maybe 90% horror and 10% disgust.

Her mother's numbers register about the same ratio.

I look down and say, "well, uh, bye you." I can't bring myself to call him Luke.

He looks back up to me with his eyes. Eyes that have already lived so much life. Heroic eyes that endured all kinds of poisons called medicines. Eyes that would never have to see a lab again.

I know he isn't able to bark, but we lock eyes and I can tell he wants to say something.

I strain my ears. And I think I can almost hear it.

'Twas in another lifetime,
one of toil and blood
When blackness was a virtue
the road was full of mud
he came in from the wilderness,
a creature void of form
Come in, I said, I'll give ya
Shelter from the storm
Come in, he said I'll give ya
Shelter from the storm

\* \* \*

We got a text two weeks later:

"Luke barked!"

**Final Moments with Bob**
*Petco Parking Lot (2020)*

Channel 96

# | seven |

# My Coming of Age

**Hilltop Apartments, Edison, NJ**
**Fourth Grade Summer (1994)**

Maybe it's this game, Super Mario 3. Yes, that must be it. That impossible desert level where the angry sun chases me relentlessly throughout.

Maybe that's why I never—

"You never go outside," my mom interrupts and turns off the bedroom TV.

*"What does he need to go outside for? Over."* rings dad from an intercom. He has just installed it in the living room to speak to the bedroom.

The only two rooms in our home.

"Because he doesn't have any friends..." mom reasons.

She waits for a response. Then realizes her mistake.

"Oh yea. Over."

"If he studies at home and gets more As, everyone will want to be his friend. Over," dad philosophizes.

*Wouldn't that be nice?*

Mom grabs my hand and walks me out of the bedroom.

We pass dad who is fidgeting with our illegal cable box and walk directly into the angry, blazing sunlight. Four kids twice my height are playing basketball—or whatever you call it when two stacked ShopRite shopping carts act as a hoop.

Negotiations are swift. My mom strikes a deal while I clutch at her hip.

I am to play basketball with these 8th graders. In return,

they can come back home for brand-name soda. But under no circumstances is Chintu, their leader, allowed to bring any paan--a kind of chewing tobacco--into the apartment.

My parents head off to the grocery store, so it is on me to somehow enforce that one and only rule.

How a 4th grader fared against these Monstars in basketball is none of your business. But we get back home and I hand them Cokes. Chintu lets out a loud burp.

> *"Do you have any candy?"*
> *"No."*
> *"Video games?"*
> *"I have Mario 3."*
> *"Mario 3? Gross. You don't have Super Nintendo?"*
> *"No."*
> *"Ugh, beer?"*

*"Shut up, chutu! you've never had beer,"* snapped one of Chintu's friend. An om tattoo rests on his forearm, drawn with a sharpie marker.

> *"Yea, dad let me try Budweiser once. Hey, what's that?"*
> *"Oh, that's our cable box."*
> *"What's a cable box?"*
> *"Oh, my dad got it. It hacks pay per view and lets us see HBO, Showtime, all that stuff for free."*

*"No. Way."*

I can see how excited they all are. Chintu grows serious.

*"What about channel 96?"*

*"Of course we have channel 96,"* I say scoffing with laughter. *"Do you guys NOT have channel 96?"*

I have no idea if we do or what that channel is.

Chintu grabs the remote. Fumbling frantically with the buttons, he finally points at the TV.

*Click.*

\* \* \*

The scene seems boring enough. A cable repairman has arrived at a lady's house. She is wearing a nightgown and, when opening the door, apologizes for not being properly dressed.

*"How dumb is she?!?"* I think. *"They give you a wide arrival window, cable guys never come on time anyway, and she's STILL not dressed?!"*

I look askance at my new friends to see if they find this as stupid as I do.

But they are transfixed. Mouths agape as if this is the greatest thing since Jurassic Park. The lady's TV is fixed in a second.

It had been unplugged.

Some dialogue follows that waxes philosophical about cable prices.

> *"Thank you so much."*
> *"Can I interest you in the premium package?"*
> *"Mhmm."*
> *"How big is that package?"*
> *"The biggest you've ever seen."*

I couldn't have been prouder of my dad who avoided this kind of useless haggling about packages and just got cable illegally.

The characters then begin to "fall in love," as my parents called it when we watched R-rated movies. They'd turn down the volume and let me play Gameboy during these performances, just boring filler between explosions or car chases.

Come to think of it, I'd never actually seen a scene like this.

Today, though, I watch it all and am amazed that these seemingly hardened 8th graders have such a romantic side to them. So I made friends and, soon, we have a routine.

We'd play what was more or less basketball and take turns stealing candy from the local convenience store. And then I provided the afternoon chick flick for these softies. It is always the same sappy formula.

Pizza delivery boy arrives. Lady has no money. They fall in love.

Candidate arrives at interview. Boss explains how competitive the market is. They fall in love.

Babysitter and boyfriend fall in love on a couch. Kid's parents find out, have a stern conversation with them. All four of them make up ... and fall in love, together.

But by Christmas, Chintu convinces his parents to get him his own cable box. And, by the summer, something called the World Wide Web begins to provide the same kinds of love stories on a computer.

They are in high school now, so I don't even get to steal candy with them anymore. Ultimately, these now-9th graders even give up our sacrosanct cart-ball to create their own love stories with the girls their age.

"What are you doing just moping around?" mom asks on a day I was feeling particularly sorry for myself. I don't want to explain that the only friends I'd had are now off being boring with girls.

That maybe if we just had Super Nintendo instead of Nintendo or Pepsi instead of Coke or better romance movies, this could have all been avoided.

"Well, what is it?"

I lie and give her something that makes sense.

"The reason I can't hang out with them ... is because they make me steal from Krauszers."

She makes me swear never to associate with them. An easy task.

I could have gone directly to Super Mario 3. Would you blame me? But something calls me outside.

Against my father's wishes of staying safe and indoors and against my mother's wishes of making friends, I step outside of our trellis and onto the sidewalk by myself.

The sun is less angry this day.

And as it shines down on my face, I realize--

This is plenty.

If you got money (yeah)
And you know it (yeah)

Then take it out your pocket;
And show it;
Then throw it like:

This-a-way; that-a-way
This-a-way; that-a-way

**Lil Wayne, Poet**
**Got Money (2008)**

# | eight |

## My Empire

**Edison, NJ, Winter 2001**

'd never been to a high school party before. Though this kind of feels like one.

I'm a senior in high school and we're in Ed Chen's finished basement. Techno music is playing.

There's the usual assortment of nerds around, like myself, but also Tracy Hazlet. She has blonde highlights and her green and gold cheerleader outfit on.

For all intents and purposes, someone like Tracy shouldn't exist. Not only is she cheer captain, but she also takes all-honors classes and has her homework done by our valedictorian-to-be. And Prabhu didn't do homework for just anybody.

But, like me, she is also in Model United Nations. So, thinking I have an 'in,' I hit her with my best line:

"Hey, do you know what this meeting's for?"

But no one knows. Though we have all been repeatedly told what this meeting isn't.

Which is to say it is definitely *not* a pyramid scheme.

Before Tracy can respond, Ed, the graduating class president, finally arrives to cheers. He walks to the middle of the basement to a green and gold podium, clearly stolen from the Student Council room, and begins his speech.

"How many of you want a nice job, a happy family, and to come home to a nice Blockbuster movie rental every night?"

It sounds really nice, actually. But everyone else is quiet, so I'm quiet.

"Well, let me tell you something. It's all a trap. Whether you work at McDonald's or as a doctor. It's all a trap."

Ed begins to then wax philosophical about web browsers.

"Internet Explorer, sucks. Netscape Navigator? I wouldn't let Netscape Navigator touch my left nutsack."

The audience is rolling all over his carpeted floor. They're all holding their stomachs as fifty or so stampeding sneakers swell to the beat of the laughter.

Presumably 2by2 Net is a browser of some kind, but maybe a PowerPoint slide is missing or something because Ed never actually explains what we are selling.

Then, he tells us how we can flip burgers or join the World Wide Web revolution. Ed had joined and now is just a few thousand dollars away from getting his Acura NSX.

There is an audible collective gasp in the room.

I am not sure what that is. As a point of reference, our family's car is a Honda Accord SE. I think the SE means we got a sunroof that opens up but sometimes doesn't close.

After 30 minutes of hearing all of Ed Chen's aspirations, we finally see what this plan would cost, 400 bucks, an impossible amount of money. And then we see the plan and how we really make money.

It is a chart of employees.

2. 4. 8. 16. 32.

Once you join, you have to get people to pay in and become employees under you. Each tier is referred to as down-1s, down-2s, etc. There is also a line straight down the middle separating the left side from the right side. And this is key because money can only be made when you complete both sides.

60 bucks for Tier 1, $100 bucks for Tier 2. $1000 for Tier 3...

The rewards got silly--in the 6-figures--the further down you went. But so did the requirement of how many people you would need to buy in. And even though we were told repeatedly this is not a pyramid scheme, the further and further down we go, the tiers ultimately make a shape best described as ... triangular.

I look around and my fellow nerds look completely different. Their eyes are filled with bloodlust. It scares me. I feel completely out of place and am hoping to get the hell out of there.

But then Ed--taking us to a fever pitch--says, "Hands up now. Are you in or are you stupid?"

I look around. Everyone's hands shoot right up. This includes Tracy's hand. And, as I look at myself, I see mine is up as well.

"You won't regret this," Ed says right after the event.

"I know, Ed. But $400 is crazy. My parents won't go for it."

He puts his arms around me, towering over me now, and says, "You know, you remind me of when I was your age."

This is a strange thing to say considering we are both seniors in high school.

He snaps his fingers. Ravi and Samir, sons of businessmen and both in Banana Republic's finest, rush over. Samir looks at me, beams a Cheshire smile, and says "you're definitely going to be my down-1!"

"I'm so...uh...down!" I shout, thinking I've made a clever pun. He comes in for a half high-five and half hug that I botch royally. But Samir doesn't seem to mind.

Ravi looks on, half-smiling, and seems to be evaluating me. As if some kind of test has concluded, he shakes my hand so firmly that I almost say, "Thank you, sir." He says I'd see them in two days and signals Samir. They hop in their respective fancy cars and drive off.

Possibly being friends with Ravi and Samir. Maybe finally getting to go to real high school parties. And Tracy Flippin' Hazlet potentially asking me ... to show her...how to use Excel?!

I feel like I'm at the beginning of a watershed moment in my life. I try to keep it cool, but I can't.

I am very happy that I raised my hand.

\* \* \*

*Two days later, in my parent's dining room.*

You see they've already given up on mom. So Ravi tries something different.

"Uncle, you'll understand this. If you wanted to start a business, what would you need?"

My dad begins to process this broad question, not sure where to begin.

"Money, right?" chimes in Ravi's down-1, Samir. "You spend some first and make more later. Just like a restaurant."

"So this is an internet restaurant?" My dad's eyebrows furrow.

*Come on, dad. Don't ruin this.*

Samir is visibly flustered. "No, what we're offering Adi is the opportunity–while he's still in high school–to buy a business and provide for both of you one day. That's what the initial money is for."

Mom starts laughing.

"Provide for us? He doesn't even know how to use stamps. You know his dad had to mail all of his college applications?"

*I want to crawl into myself.*

"Look," Ravi takes over. His voice gets low.

"It's obvious you both care about your son. And applying to all of those colleges clearly means he must be bright. We all already know he's smarter than me and Samir. We just really think he can also become a leader."

I start to choke up.

*Is this the vision my new friends have for me?*

I can't hear much else of what is said. You see, like a true leader, I am overhearing this conversation from the steps to my room. My parents don't want me interfering.

So, before this leader embarks on his million dollar idea, he'll need his parent's approval.

And 400 bucks.

After Ravi and Samir leave, I plead with my parents. It is a pathetic sight. It is the kind of pleading that fully informs how I never kissed a girl in high school.

"Ok, neither of us like this plan, but we want you to fail and see how hard it is to make one dollar into two." My mom's inspiring words reveal a crack in the glacier.

My dad looks at me.

His first job in America was putting on a tie as a life insurance salesman for Metlife in the late 80s. But everyone viewed him as an outsider: his coworkers and his prospects who hung up on him. This left his small Indian community of friends and family as his only potential clients.

And so my father went around Edison, NJ, papers in hand, reminding his loved ones of how they could die at any moment. That's how he put food on the table.

I'd learn later that he despised everything about that job.

But today, he doesn't have many words. "Merry early Christmas,' he says. "Let me know how it works out."

And, with that, and 400 bucks, I set out to become a titan of the World Wide Web.

* * *

Because I joined so quickly—and perhaps because there might be a God—it is none other than Tracy that becomes my left-side down-1. Within a week, her friends–three cheerleaders, two dancers and the only attractive color guard–sign up and fill out the left half of my down-2 and down-3.

Within a month, Ed Chen purchases his NSX and announces that the 2by2Net founder will be speaking at the Hilton in Times Square.

"Yes, the Times Square in New York City," Ed patiently explains to a starry-eyed down-4 whose middle school-ness is showing. My team and I look at each other and know we have a huge opportunity to prepare for.

\* \* \*

The train ride into the city is something to behold. Ravi, Samir and I are flanked by a fleet of cheerleaders, dancers, and flag wavers, all new prospects.

From the window, I see the NYC skyline. To me, this is the dream or at least is quickly becoming the dream. Going on business meetings. Wearing fancy suits. Seemingly uncapped success. All as a high schooler. And this isn't something depressing like life insurance. This is a real tech company. I'd even started learning about Acuras and figuring out which ones really spoke to me as an individual.

I decide to treat the team to lunch beforehand at a nice restaurant in the heart of Wall Street. I know we'll have to take a subway, that it is far out of our way from Times Square and that it will cost me money I don't have, but it feels important to walk past that giant metal bull, a symbol we've arrived.

After some quick research into restaurant prices, we settle on a Panera just outside of Wall Street.

Sufficiently souped and sandwiched, we scuttle back to the subway to head to Times Square. I am the last to swipe my ticket through when two things become clear: the train is arriving and I have insufficient fare.

I look at the turnstile, the gaggle of attractive girls waiting for me, the business meeting I have to attend. Should this meaningless $1.25 fare stop an empire?

So, I hop the turnstile.

An undercover Giuliani-era cop rises out of a group of homeless people and immediately apprehends me. There is a flurry of harsh words. I am stunned. This large trunchbull of a female cop eventually breaks her rhythm when she realizes I am catatonic.

"Do you even speak English?"

I see an out if I can look like a deer-in-headlights new immigrant but it will be time-consuming. Time that we don't have. I also see Tracy looking at me with vague concern or mild annoyance. At the time, it is probably the greatest moment in my life.

With a flair for the dramatic, I start breathing again, look at Tracy in the distance and say:

"You need to go on."

(dramatic pause)

"Go on without me."

She leaves without protest.

"You do speak English!" And a fine of $76.45 is written out.

As I am getting my fine, I see Ravi, Samir, Tracy and her friends all hop on the subway. No one waits around. No one even looks back. And as the subway train passes by, I think I see them through the window, all laughing without a care in the world.

I hop on the next 2,3 train to catch up to them. But as the train pulls into the stop right before, Penn Station, I hop off. This is the stop that can connect me back onto a New Jersey train. And I don't feel like there is anything there for me in Times Square.

So I make my way back directly to New Jersey rife with fines and Panera debt.

I am in my ill-fitting dad's suit with a tie that is barely on that I don't know how to adjust. And I must look like I need help.

"Hey, what's wrong, brother?"

A man in a leather jacket with slicked back hair and an emaciated face--picture a Steve Buscemi if he was really poor--sits down next to me on the train.

I don't know why, but I tell him every last bit of detail leaving all stones turned, even the bit about the turnstile ticket and what a loser I felt like.

"You know, your parents won't find out about that ticket if you send a money order."

He is my guardian angel.

My new companion also feels this advice is worth $10 and it becomes clear there'll be no opportunity to negotiate this.

I get back to Edison and drive right to the 7-Eleven. The convenience store attendant patiently explains how to get the money order. He also uncomfortably explains how to mail it.

I'd never used a stamp before.

\* \* \*

That Monday, I find out that Ed Chen and the 2by2Net founder had been arrested and both walked through Times Square in handcuffs. Everyone else was detained and my entire team was fined heavily.

A detective eventually tracks me down in school. I am in tears the entire walk to the principal's office.

You see, Ravi and Samir would bounce back. They have their dads' businesses and connections to fall back on. And Tracy would likely have many Prabhus in her life doing her work for her.

*But what about me? All those quizzes and tests are about to become worthless pieces of paper. I've never been to a real party. Oh god. What will I tell my parents?*

"Merry Early Christmas, Adi," begins to repeat and throb in my head.

It all feels so unfair and it makes me sick to my stomach.

The detective opens up the door for me. I take a few quick short breaths and he walks me into the principal's office.

The detective starts:

"This company, if you can call it that, 2by2 Net. What do they sell?"

"Uh--"

"Nothing."

He hands me a landscape-oriented sheet and points to a spot.

"Tell me who's that right there"

"Well, that's--"

"… yea, that's you."

There are a lot more dubiously rhetorical questions like this.

So I just keep my eyes on the sheet. It shows Tracy, my left side down-1, then her down-2s, and 3s. My embarrassingly empty right side also stares back at me. It shows the vast network of up-1s, 2s, 3s, 4s and beyond. Even Ed Chen, larger than life, is just one tiny dot there with way more people above him.

"Let me ask you this once, are you going to sign anyone else onto 2by2 Net?"

I wait for the rhetorical coast to clear.

"No."

"Good," the principal jumps in now. "You see all those people there, son. Those are all kids and this scam has cost them and our town almost half a million dollars."

He hands me his box of tissues, which I need.

I wait for what I know will come next.

But it doesn't.

Apparently, because I had only filled out my left side and failed at signing any non-cheerleaders, I have not made a cent of profit.

This makes me a victim and not a suspect. I am offered the opportunity to join a class action and leave with the box of tissues, a brochure, and no punishment.

Well, almost no punishment.

\* \* \*

A week later, my parents get a strange receipt from the New York Metro Transit Authority.

"We're disappointed you didn't tell us about this ticket," frowns dad as he fidgets with the VCR to get Home Alone to work.

"I just can't believe this idiot learned how to send mail," scoffs mom. "Merry Christmas" are her final words as she shoves a hot chocolate with marshmallows on top in my hands, angrily.

I look at them, my real left and right Up-1s, and realize there are no shortcuts.

And this is the only empire I'll ever need.

**The Finer Things**
*Tarascon, France (2019)*

# | nine |

## My Preserve

**Newark Airport, Terminal C (2019)**

"Where's the 12th one." my wife says, more a statement than a question.

"Um...the twelfth of what?"

Using my plastic fork–a particularly cheap airport varietal–I poke my nachos around and try to avoid all eye contact.

"What else are we bringing a dozen boxes of to Europe?!" Melissa snaps and opens the blue duffle towards me.

The truth is ... I know the truth.

And I am not proud.

* * *

Two months ago, my estranged childhood friend, Damien, whom I haven't seen in 12 years, invited us to his wedding.

*At a villa. In the South of France.*

This unreal trip is a reminder that when your friends write "K.I.T. xoxo" in your middle school yearbook, it might be a good idea to actually keep in touch.

*I mean, it could mean a villa. In the South of France.*

And the only gift Damien asked us to bring was ourselves. But it felt criminal to bring nothing.

*After all, did I mention this wedding was at a villa? And was in the South of France?*

So we pushed further. Damien finally broke and confessed that there was in fact something that we could bring.

A single box of Pop Tarts.

Somewhere, resting on idle but immutable in Damien's clouded childhood memory of America, was a profound love for an edible breakfast pastry–edible if we're being generous with our compliments.

And it was a request so pure of heart, so charming, and so confusing, that I went to the nearest pharmacy that day and bought 12 boxes. One box for every year we'd spent apart.

12 boxes.

Each box held 4 packets.

Each packet held two Pop Tarts.

Some back-of-the-napkin math would tell you there were 96 Pop Tarts in total.

That meant I would have to show self-control for two months while 96 Pop Tarts–some even s'more-flavored–sat in our pantry.

\* \* \*

"Well?"

My wife splays the blue duffel open and gestures it towards me. Eleven--frankly accusatory--boxes stare back at me, looking angry but organized. I pretend to focus on the Newark Airport departures screen, still a few hours from our flight.

"Honestly, he probably wouldn't like the s'more flavor," I explain limply.

Mel looks back at me, unimpressed. "And what about the Eiffel Tower?"

She is right.

$4 + 3 + 2 + 1$ would have made a triangle out of ten boxes. 2 more at the top for the spire. At the wedding, I was going to hashtag the Facebook photo "#LaTarteEiffel."

Now my Tarte Eiffel is just a pyramid pitching a tiny chub.

Which reminds me, Damien hasn't commented on my photo of the blue duffel I took when we arrived at the airport. I shoot a Whatsapp text to him to check his Facebook.

A response arrives.

"Hey Adi! So excited you're able to make it to the wedding. Quick request, Elo and I aren't putting our pictures of the wedding on social media. If you could try to not post any photos during the wedding, I would appreciate it."

I twitch as I read it, feeling like my wrist has been slapped.

"That's enough nachos," Melissa says and slaps my wrist more literally.

I swirl my thoughts around about Damien's request on the red eye over. But the international flight's free beer and wine and the ticking clock slowly put me to bed along with happy thoughts.

*A villa in the South of France, wow. Just wow.*
*Why don't they just call it Southern France or South France?*
*You don't hear anyone say 'I'm visiting the South of Pole!'*
*Hehe, South of Pole. I bet she'd like to visit South of Pole .*
*Heyoooo...*

And that is my final deep thought of the day.

\* \* \*

We arrive at the wedding the next day. Mel and I look at each other and just lose it.

Olive trees cascade across the entire property. Old stone castles bathe in daylight. Bountiful cheese trays lay out in the summer sun. Horses draw guests to and from the property.

We've arrived a day early to help Damien, Elo, and their friends working on setup.

I embrace Damien who is much more bearded than I remember. My wife immediately ingratiates herself to the friend group with her knowledge of flower arrangements. Knowing nothing of this world, I sit and strip leaves off branches with my fingers to make confetti for the wedding ceremony.

It is a pathetic scene as I sit hunched over and alone. A quasi-Quasimodo.

When my hands start to get raw, I switch to drinking wine and taking photos of the flower arrangements being assembled.

*I've interpreted Damien's request as "photos are ok just don't post them on social media."*

The next morning is the ceremony.

Though my middle school French could only pick up the first three words, "Madames et Monsieurs," I take video of the entire procession.

And as they walk out to their carriage, my single hand with calloused fingers raises above the crowd and uses the phone to slow-motion capture the leaves flying through the air.

The leaves add jagged edges to rounded, smiling faces and stick firmly to those with not-so-dry eyes. Myself included.

At the cocktail hour, sea snails, oysters, Cuban cigars, and chocolate fountains are sprinkled throughout. Perfect for macros/portrait mode shots.

Dinner's table assignments are identified with polaroids of you and the groom or bride. I pick up the picture of me and Damien from 12 years ago and hold our younger selves in my hand.

He's smiling back clearly at me without his current beard. I'm brandishing a giant Knicks foam finger outside Madison Square Garden, also beardlessly. With a quick sleight of hand, I take a quick photo of the photo before anyone can see.

I memorialize the inside jokes and wedding speeches at dinner with video and that leads us to the night, which is complete bacchanalia.

Around 6am, only **halfway** through the dancing, the wedding party starts handing out masks. I am at that stage in the evening where every thought I have is a brilliant one. So I take a Super Mario face, grab Damien's best man, Ben, and explain my idea to him.

We go into the bathroom. I take off my shirt and he helps me re-button it with the buttons going up my back. We put the Mario face on the back of my head so it looks like my front.

My back/Mario's front dances the night away while my front/me converses with the wallflowers through cigar smoke and an *eau de* what is mostly rum.

"Would've been a cool video," I think, but my shirt has become a strait jacket of sorts making it difficult to access my phone.

\* \* \*

There is a poolside brunch the next morning, most of which is a blur, having only slept from 10am to 10:45am.

We say our goodbyes and then commence the long flight home, exhausted and happy.

When I get home, I begin to miss our new friends in a way that makes my heart race. Clutching my phone, I start swiping through the photos, starting from the last day's poolside shots.

Here are all these peculiar creatures, playing boardgames on a board with just 6 people instead of teaming up globally on a virtual island to kill 100s with a shovel.

In that other photo, they are eating fine cheeses and beautiful homemade breads. But they rip off pieces of both and toss their food onto napkins in a haphazard and completely un-Instagrammable fashion.

And their strange smiles and laughter are always a cacophony of asymmetrical notes. Why are their heads always tilted back, impossible for me to get a flattering angle of them?

A sinking feeling takes over me.

*What is this moment in time and what is the point of all these photos? Will I ever meet these people again?*

My existential meltdown is rudely interrupted by a Whatsapp message.

"Hey Adi, it was awesome having you come for the wedding and partying together until sunrise! We were also touched by your gift. For sure we will do our best to see you next summer in the USA. Take care. Hugs and kisses to you both."

I see Damien is still typing.

"Oh, Ben also made you this gif."

It is of me and Mario me dancing, perfectly clipped as if I am dancing forever.

Then a second photo comes in.

In the foreground, Damien holds one box of Pop Tarts and what I assume is a smile behind his beard.

In the background is a 3+2+1 triangle with a 1, 1, 1 spire. As I count them up, including the one in his hand, I realize the eleventh box is already missing.

I start laughing out loud with no one around.

"Don't eat them all at once," I text back, holding back tears. "They can last basically forever."

Three dots appear indicating Damien is typing.

The dots disappear.

It feels like forever.

But then a message appears.

"K.I.T. xoxo"

**clockwise: groom + mom in carriage; La Tarte Eiffel;
Mario-back dancing w/ groom; a younger Damien and me
captured**

"The thing is, Bob, it's not that I'm lazy, it's that I just don't care ...

Eight (bosses), Bob. So that means when I make a mistake, I have eight different people coming by to tell me about it.

That's my only real motivation is not to be hassled; that, and the fear of losing my job.

But you know, Bob, that will only make someone work just hard enough not to get fired."

*Office Space (1999)*

# | ten |

# My Big Idea

You could have been doomscrolling through the internet or swiping right on some pretty people, but you chose to be here today instead. So thank you all for coming and taking out some time to hear me.

So I have this big idea.

You want to hear about it?

Well, I can tell you, but you **have** to promise not to tell anyone.

Seriously.

In fact, this is so serious that I'm hoping you'll repeat after me:

"I promise"

*waits for you to say "I promise"

"Not to"

*Waits for you to say "not to"

"Disclose any confidential information except to those employees who are required to have the Confidential information in order to perform their job duties in connection with the limited purposes of this agreement."

Go ahead. I'll wait.

\* \* \*

Perfect. Now I think you know how serious this is.

And I'm a straight shooter, honestly it's my greatest weakness, so we should probably start on the idea, right?

The idea involves the internet. The potential is through the roof.

So, well — It's actually a little harder to explain without some of the background. The background is actually very important, so let me give you some context.

Where should we begin?

\* \* \*

So about a year ago, I was on a toilet. Trust me, it's important.

This wasn't just any toilet. This one was special as it was the first and the last time I'd be on the toilet of the Shravana Bhavan in Edison, New Jersey.

Shravana Bhavan is a great South Indian restaurant chain in general, but I would steer clear of the one in Edison. That is, unless you want to wind up taking residence in the same place I am in this story.

But I mention this toilet because that was where my big idea struck me.

So I flush and hurry back to Melissa.

"Eureka!" I shout.

"You reek, ugh" my girlfriend at the time, now wife, responds.

She's a straight shooter too.

I explain that the idea involves the internet. That the potential is through the roof.

And so we plan out our lives and how we'll make room for our big idea.

What would we call the company? What would the logo look like? What kind of house should we get? I'm partial to being inside the city as much as possible.

My counterpoint's desires include chickens and buying land for said chickens to do whatever chickens do.

We talk about what our family should look like. She says she wants three kids. I'm an only child and feel surprisingly normal enough to promote that upbringing.

And so we spend the whole dinner discussing everything surrounding the big idea.

Then go to the bathroom.

And then discuss the idea some more.

But, enough about the digestions...and digressions.

We should get to the actual idea, right? Sorry, I'm a straight shooter, so let's get to the point.

As I said, the idea involves the Internet. And the potential is through the roof.

And, I think you'll soon agree that the scalability is what makes it so very attractive.

So...

\* \* \*

Well, actually, it might be useful to go further back. Because the motivation behind starting this company is almost just as important as the idea itself.

I assure you it's not money or something uninspiring like that. Too often founders get caught up in an idea for the wrong reasons.

You see I grew up with two very honest and lovable parents.

They always tell me to "work hard at whatever you do. And if what you do happens to be becoming a doctor, we'll buy you a car."

And my friends all grew up to follow this path more or less.

But I was never good at memorizing things. This is a problem. It's why I read stories off my Kindle today and it's why I wasn't the greatest student. But I have these ideas from time to time. And they always die on the vine.

My motivation is to show that there's another way for those of us who aren't traditionally smart. Which reminds me, the idea!

Let's get to that!

\* \* \*

Oh, but one more thing.

I've always had trouble with authority. This would be an opportunity for anyone that's ever hated their boss. Found them completely uninspired. Out for themselves. Unwilling to make a bold move. We don't want people like that. If they exist in our company, they won't rise past mailroom clerk.

Ok so the idea and it's crazy upside...

Oh, a final note about what we'll be doing with the money.

\* \* \*

Charity. You can be a good person and still create a fortune. Giving back is not only important, but it's what will make us different and better than those around us.

You've all been really patient. So, my idea is.

\* \* \*

It's.

\* \* \*

It's um.

One second.

\* \* \*

Stupid memory.

\* \* \*

Well this is embarrassing.

Sorry for taking up your time.

Sorry for wasting time.

It was a big idea though.

I swear.

The idea involves the internet. The potential is through the roof.

# $875 Luxurious Apartment Room for breakneck price

Hello, I have read your posting on Craiglist. I am an international student from Germany studying political science at AU...

Hi, I'm mid-20s professional in DC for work.

Roomie, I'm 28 year old, 5"6', straight, single, and nice. Mailing from Hawaii.

Hey, This may be the best apartment ever!! I'm 27 from Bombay starting at Georgetown in the fall.

Hey there, Does the fee include any utilities? *(name redacted); USAID Program*...

Hi, I'm at Booz Allen Hamilton + a swimmer (How big is the lap pool?)

Helooo, Is my room the living room or an actual room?...

# | eleven |

## My Left Han

**Washington, DC (2009)**

He was a star athlete in basketball and football. I thought table tennis was a sport.

Ladies would buy *him* shots at the bar. I once worked up the courage to ask the prettiest girl in my class—if *she* wanted to borrow *my* notes.

He had a magnetic personality that would draw in our peers by the hundreds.

And I had magnet Bittorrent links, downloading movies by the hundreds . . . of kilobytes . . . per second.

\* \* \*

And so in my second year in law school, when Vinay asks me to be his roommate, I am beside myself. Sure, we have our differences, but it is our similarities that bring us together.

Chief amongst them, we want to live in the fanciest building in Washington, DC but at a cheaper rent than all our friends. Our sights are set upon the Alban Towers.

The building has everything we need. Inspired by the National Cathedral across the street, stone gargoyles adorn the entrance, a grand piano greets you in the lobby, and the roof overlooks all of DC. The common area is massive—easily accommodating Vinay's attractive friends. And it has free wireless, which I hope to magnify to ensure our apartment has free wireless.

As for the apartment, the jewel in the crown is a very thin hallway that leads to our massive living room; or as we'd come to call it, the third bedroom.

Converting the living room into a bedroom allows us to "ghetto the system," a verb we create early in our friendship.

Ghettoing the room thus brings our individual rents well below $1000 a month.

And so begins our revolving door of interesting living room roommates—or the "others" as we soon begin calling them—*Lost* is a popular show at this time. There is Quiet Milosh who works for the state department. He never speaks a word to us but we can hear him on the phone from midnight to 2am speaking a harsh foreign language. He uses a pocketknife to cut vegetables and sleeps covered in an elaborate blanket—red, white and blue adorned with a two-headed white eagle.

Our imagination runs wild. Perhaps Quiet Milosh is a mason whose ancestors helped build America.

We later find out the blanket is the flag of Serbia. This leads to a new house rule. If any potential DC roommates say they work for the government, we now are sure to ask "which one?"

There are roommates with funny names like Joyful Stream, a Caucasian girl who attempts to teach two Indian kids from New Jersey about the body's natural chakras, or as Joyful would pronounce: "shakras." Others try to sneak in pets.

But the one I will always keep close to my heart is Han.

Han is from South Korea and has just emigrated to the United States to become a French chef. Vinay and I would be his first experience living with Americans. Our interview of him is swift.

We are about to gain a roommate who wants to cook dinner for us every day, is willing to pay a higher rent than either of us, and agrees to divide the living room in half—one as his bedroom and the other half as a common space. The common area is ostensibly for us all to have dinner together but will later become a pre-party drinking haven for Vinay, his attractive groupies, and me.

Han's only caveat is, and I quote, "At 4 am, I have to wake up and sharpen my knives." Once he moves in, we sleep right through the knife-sharpening and marvel at his unimaginable routine.

Han works in his French restaurant from 4:30 am to 9:30 pm and arrives home at 10 pm only to begin cooking the next day's dinner for Vinay and me. While he cooks, Vinay and I drink boxed wine and give Han our not-so-gourmand feedback on how he can improve on our prior meal. Han falls asleep around 10:30 pm, the sounds of Vinay and I playing NBA Jam cutting through a thin chiffon Japanese folding wall that separates him from us.

Word spreads around the law school, Vinay and Adi have an indentured immigrant who barely speaks English living in a corner of their living room who cooks for them and for no pay. The optics do not look good, but what scares me the most about this rumor is that most of it is true. In fact, the only thing that isn't true is what little credit they give to Han's English.

But such a thing is not meant to last. A few months into Han's stay, I get the call.

"He left."

"What?"

"He Han. Han left, bro."

I'd seen 7 missed calls from Vinay and have called him back after finishing my Constitutional Law class.

"What do you mean he left? He leaves every day. He sharpens his knives and he leaves."

"No dude. He left. He's gone. There's a note on the floor near your door. I can only read some of it but I can't pick it up. You need to come here right now, bro."

I drive back home and walk up to the building. The gargoyles jeer back at me as I pass through the entrance. Vinay has injured himself playing basketball earlier in the month and is in a cast and crutches. I realize this is why he can't pick up the note from the ground.

I perform this most remedial of tasks for my athletic role model and read the note aloud to the both of us. It is in Han's most formal attempt at English.

"Atidya and Viney, I feel very sorry for you guys. Mom came from Korea and saw me. We packed and leave today. I hope I remember you both. Security deposit is yours. The future is yours. Next time we see each other; I hope to cut you something nice. Han."

*So maybe his English was as bad as the rumors.*

"The future is ours?" I ask and hand the letter to Vinay.

"I think he meant furniture."

And that is the last we ever see of Han.

\* \* \*

As karma would have it, I graduate in 2010 and arrive into a job market that is unforgiving. At first, I refuse to give in, move into the very same living room and take on every odd job I can find—somehow convincing myself that holding a clipboard outside the DC Metro is legal advocacy.

All my slick attempts to ghetto the system end in me just ghettoing myself. Eventually, I realize it is time to return home to New Jersey.

On that last day in DC, I can't help but think of Han.

He single-mindedly chased a dream regardless of what it cost or who might be taking advantage of him along the way.

It's a simple lesson in the end: when the going gets tough, get up early, sharpen your knives and know when it's time to move on.

Because the future is yours.

**urbandictionary = the only time I've been published**

*Oh, wait, almost forgot to count this book!*

# (Recipe) Fluffiest Pancakes of All Time

Other than McDonald's "Hot Cakes," there's no such thing as a bad pancake. So why rock the boat?

Well, a pancake is good. A fluffy pancake is best. And the Fluffiest Pancake of All Time is even bester! (Yes, when you make the FPOAT, grammar breaks.)

So follow your usual recipe but then:

1. When making your own pancake mix, include baking powder and baking soda.
2. When mixing ingredients, fold them in, don't beat heavily. And stop when consistency is like oatmeal, as opposed to an even paste.
3. When adding milk or water, replace ½ of this liquid with club soda (Add the club soda after most of the mixing/stirring is complete)
4. When flipping, cover the pan for 15-20 seconds to allow steam to rise pancakes further.

You don't have to sacrifice crunch. A well-greased/buttered pan allows for texture on the outside and fluff in the middle. Enjoy and--as you'll soon be encouraged to do in the next story--remember to serve others first...

**We can make pancakes**

# | twelve |

## My Whisper

**Baltimore, Maryland (Fall 2002)**

A lion floats through the air.

*I swear this feels like it's happening in slow motion.*

A lamb then takes flight in a perfect arc in the opposite direction. And when the lion makes its way back down to Earth, a bull hurtles off in pursuit of the lamb.

Like a perfectly synced clock, on it went like this, over and over again.

This is a typical sight on the quad. During that first se-mester of college, I would walk to the same morning behav-ioral psych class. And on these mornings, there would be Ashish, juggling beanie babies.

As he juggles and walks, on the back of Ashish's shoulder is a deer. While I'd never admit it to my friends, I know the name of that one–Whisper. I had a Whisper at home and this Whisper would stare right into my soul daily.

You see, I would always keep a safe distance behind Ashish. This is not out of any fear of a juggling mishap, but out of the social suicide that would follow being accidentally affiliated with the juggler who had no friends. And a few yards back puts me right in the deer's line of sight.

So on it went like this, at 7:30 in the morning, every Monday, Wednesday, and Friday. It is probably wrong that I never said hi, but I always have the best excuses:

1. *Well, if I spoke to Ashish, I'd be leaving my roommate alone who has abandonment issues.*
2. *Ashish might think that I'm only speaking to him because he's Indian, so I don't want to be reductionist. And ...*
3. *Oh, it's best leave him alone. Ashish probably is one of those people that is 'introverted' and needs his space.*

*Abandonment, reductionist, introverted.* All words I pick up from this psych class and brandish three times a week.

But, eventually, I start to feel bad. I mean, in class, this is a guy who sits at his desk and arranges Star Wars figurines in some kind of pep rally around himself. Yoda is cheer captain and Han's on the bleachers.

So one day while he is juggling, I say "hey" and put my hand on Ashish's non-deer-occupied shoulder. This is a mistake.

All the animals hit the marble and brick road and Ashish begins screaming.

Loud. Hysterical. Feral.

I apologize profusely and bend down to pick up his fallen soldiers. This is another mistake. I am shoved out of the way. Not lightly, either, as I find myself rolled onto the grass area.

He picks up his toys himself and starts repeating "Roary. Snort. Fleece," over and over.

"Roary. Snort. Fleece."

*It is the names of his lion, bull, and lamb.*

A number of morning class-goers begin laughing at the

scene. One lacrosse player shouts from across the quad "no means no" and *consoles* Ashish by informing him that there's "plenty of cuter boys in the sea." Ashish keeps shouting his mantra and starts running away.

Their laughter echoes off the four buildings in the quad and eventually wanes. "Roary. Snort. Fleece." gets dimmer and Ashish gets smaller in the distance.

I am left with my own thoughts. Our psych textbook would likely describe them as "anger" and "embarrassment."

Naturally, I make sure I have nothing to do with *him* for the rest of the semester.

As we approach finals we come to our study week. The first day is usually designated for hanging out at the "Beach," a misnomer that is in fact a large grass area in front of the library at our rather landlocked university.

Since it is a Tuesday, I am at the Beach making plans with friends for--not *if*--but *when* we'll be going to PJs. This local bar is just across the street and sits in the basement of my apartment building. Their $2.50 deal nets you three tacos and two Coronas, so it made little sense to drink anywhere else or do anything else on a Tuesday afternoon.

Then, in the distance, I see Ashish and my jaw nearly drops. He is carrying a "paper" airplane–in quotes because it is so large that it comes up to his shoulders, needs two hands to be carried, and is made entirely out of sheet metal.

As he walks through the Beach, he draws more and more attention. I am not sure when I realize that he's coming towards me, but it must have clearly been too late.

"You want to help me install this?" he asks me nonchalantly in front of nearly a thousand underclassmen.

"No. Oh my god. No." I say loud enough for many to hear. I pull him to the outskirts of the throng.

"Why are you even asking me?" I whisper.

I look around. Like a true thespian, I gesticulate wildly and widely to show everyone how shocked I am and how irregular this conversation is.

"Oh, because you're my friend" is his matter-of-fact response. He continues past me and settles on some lonely patch of turf.

I head off to PJs.

8 beers, 12 tacos, and only ten dollars later, I fall out of the bar into a crisp early December evening. The noisy lot of us are headed to a friend's place to cheer him up over a breakup and, of course, play Mariokart at his house.

In the distance, I see a glowing white orb on the Beach. As my eyes come into focus–slowly of course–I can see the the outline of the paper airplane.

The tip digs into the ground and the rest hangs in the air, as if the child of a 50 foot giant forgot to clean up after play-time. Even from this distance I can make out the light blue college-ruled lines. It is a three-hole punched paper. Two of the holes hides in the folds and the other is visible on the left wing from even this distance.

It makes me smile.

And, later that night, I can see it from my bedroom win-dow. The Coronas have worn off and it is the most beautiful thing I've ever seen.

\* \* \*

The Friday after Taco Tuesday is the big Psychology final. Today is Thursday, the day before, so I finally open the text-book for the first time. Somewhere around 3am, I hit a chap-ter entirely about Ashish.

The outbursts. The attention to detail. The need for repetitive motion. He makes just a little bit more sense.

The next morning, he is out in the middle of the freshman quad, with a George Foreman grill, serving pancakes. Everyone coming out receives two and he stages an area where you can pour syrup.

Assuming he is a cafeteria employee, most don't acknowledge him as they are handed free food. I know it might go south but I try speaking to him again.

*"What are you doing?"*

*"Making pancakes."*

*"Right, but why?"*

*"I observed that during finals week, people weren't eating breakfast. So I'm making them some."*

*"But don't you have our psych final coming up?"*

*"They give me a lot of extra time but I don't need it."*

It is simple for him yet otherworldly to me. But that was that.

\* \* \*

I'd like to tell you that we became best friends or that we learned to understand each other better or that when the bullies and lions came, I protected him from it like one of his Star Wars idols.

It was only a matter of time before something really bad happened to Ashish. And when it did, I didn't do anything, behaving as limp as Whisper on his shoulder.

I'll never understand how Ashish saw the world or how he willingly threw himself into his passions without a care for the judgment that would follow.

But he's a painful reminder that we aren't powerless and we can do some good around us.

We might never be heroes, but, damn it, maybe we can walk together?

We can make pancakes.

## INTERMISSION

*Please consume or dispose of all drinks and snacks before returning to your seats.*

PART TWO

# (Recipe) Mom's CheeseDosa Recipe

## *(Makes 10-12 dosas)*

---

### DAY ONE

- 2 Cups Long Grain Rice
- 1 Cup Urad Daal (Split Matpe Beans)
- 1/4 Teaspoon Whole Fenugreek Seeds
- 3-4 chopped chillies in olive oil *(Day Three)*
- Mexican Blend cheese *(Day Three)*

Wash and then soak the rice and the urad daal in **separate** containers. Let rest overnight 8-9 hours.

*(Matpe beans available on Amazon)*

# DAY TWO

In the morning...

First, grind the **Urad Daal** to a smooth consistency by adding enough water to ensure smooth grinding. However, it should **not** get so diluted where it takes on a pouring consistency. Remove and place in large vessel.

Next, grind **Long Grain Rice** to a smooth consistency. Add small amounts of the overnight soaked water to the ground rice batter. Add this and **Fenugreek Seeds** to your Urad Daal mixture and mix thoroughly. Drape cheesecloth or something breathable over the mix.

**Reminder:** This should be in a large bowl as the batter is going to rise.

Keep bowl in the hottest part of your house. As this sits, a wild yeast ferment will take place for 24 hours. If you complete these steps in the morning, the dosas will be ready to serve for breakfast the next day (Day Three).

*In South India, dosas are often a breakfast/brunchtime food. However, the savory, spongy, crunchy, and slightly tart flavors make it a perfectly fine lunch or dinner option. Whenever you decide to eat it, time the 24-hour rise accordingly.*

# DAY THREE

Congratulations, your batter has risen!

Mix thoroughly. Then, take a portion in a smaller bowl. Add a pinch of salt to taste and enough water for an easy-pour consistency.

*Getting the right consistency may take some failed tries just like the first time you made pancakes. Don't be too hard on yourself here.*

Ensure your pan is hot. Wipe the surface with a tissue paper soaked in high-heat oil. Take 1/4 cup or so of batter and pour onto middle of pan. Working quickly, with bottom of a ladle, spread mixture evenly going from middle to outer rings in a spiraling continuous motion. Little to no pressure, let gravity do the work.

After some browning, add desired levels of **Mexican Cheese**. Once melted, layer in **Chopped Chillies**.

When removing the dosa, you can fold it like a crepe. But extra points go to brave souls that roll it into a cylindrical shape. This allows the heat to remain in but any condensation to leave, keeping things crispy.

# NOTES

Batter keeps 3-4 days in fridge // month in freezer.

I eat it with a spicy mix of Malga Pudi and olive oil as well as a pat of butter with a spoon of sugar on top. I'm the only one who does this. You will likely eat your dosa traditionally with **Coconut Chutney** and **Sambhar.**

What else.

Oh, I should probably let you know that CheeseDosa is a metaphor for how I've never felt like I belonged anywhere--not in India or America. This could have made me feel suffocating isolation or deep inadequacy. But I had a mom who let me live freely. To put anything on my dosa.

Now, my love of something as American as cheese and something as Indian as dosa gives me a stake in something truly unique. Something delicious. Something better than the sum of its parts. Something that I not only proudly say is mine ...

... but gives me a sense of belonging.

*CheeseDosas can be a little heavy. Pair with mimosas.*

**Mom's Dosa-Making Class**
*July 2020*

"Do you know what today is?"

**Kirti Surendran to her son**
**... at 6:30am**
*... on Makar Sankranti*
*... or Maha Shivaratri*
*... or some other obscure Hindu holiday*
(1988-Present)

# | thirteen |

# My Clarification

So, growing up, like many of you, there were the names we had for things while we were at home and then, at school, there were the new "outside" names we would learn for those same things.

I am eight when I first begin to appreciate the difference between these names. I have recently fallen in love with mom's bhindi and want to explain the wonders of it to my other friends.

"So it's green all over ... and ... it's a vegetable, you know? It's gooey, but, like, good gooey. Stop looking at me like that.

It's just awesome. AND! When you cut it up you get these stars that you can stick on your face. The stars stick to your face!"

And that's when it happens.

"Oh, do you mean okra?"

Some know-it-all amongst my friends says something like this about halfway through my excitement. There always seems to be some new name for just about anything I eat at home.

"Guys, seriously. Kulfi is this whole different kind of ice cream. It kind of melts differently though. It looks like a tiny jousting stick and is delicious."

"Oh, I think that's just frozen condensed milk."

"Ok. Ok. So. We put this stuff on our basmati rice. It's called dahi and–"

"Oh, I'm pretty sure you mean long-grain rice. And you're talking about yogurt…thinned out with some water."

I hate this kid, through and through. It isn't really just one kid, but I hate this composite of smartasses in my life.

Something I think is magical, Indian and unique invariably gets reduced down to some stupid name like long grain rice or cilantro. But I try to be reasonable. If these items are actually used in America and have simply been given their own name here, I can learn to deal with that. To each their own naming conventions, after all.

I would scour the aisles of the supermarket just to make sure these American names truly exist for the things I ate at home. There is the okra in the produce section. There is the condensed milk in the cans aisle. And, yes, there is the box of long-grain rice with a bearded old black man on the cover smiling peacefully right back at me.

But the superiority of it all still upsets me.

"Oh, Adi, do you *mean* okra?"

"No, Daniel. Actually, I *mean* bhindi. And you know why I mean bhindi? Guess why? … Because I said bhindi! … if I meant okra I would've said okra you presumptuous sonnofa-"

\* \* \*

So, yes, I seethe about this throughout most of my formative years. And anything that is actually unique to my house and didn't have some stupid outside name usually tastes too gross to actually brag about. There is no American name for karela, a devastatingly bitter gourd.

"It's good for your blood!!!" mom can be found yelling

weekly while chasing a scampering version of me who has realized what's for dinner.

And Indian sweets, not much better-tasting than karela, also don't have Americanized names. "It's like a really soggy munchkin," I say, halfheartedly, getting a friend to try gulab jamun for the first time.

I am losing hope but then realize the answer is so clear and so obvious. It has been with me at nearly every meal and is a source of tremendous pride.

Ghee.

Of course! Ghee!

Ghee is the alpha and the omega of Indian cuisine. It makes things taste good in a way that butter could only dream of. Is your naan too dry or your rice too boring? Ghee. Is your veggies too devastatingly bitter? Ghee! ... Did you have a bad day? GHEE!

I couldn't wait to tell my friends. When Monday hits, I hurry off to school.

"Gather around, my people," I say to our table of nerds in fifth period lunch.

"So, listen. There's this thing we have. It's liquid gold that melts when hot.  It's like an oily, wax butter thing that makes other things taste amazing.  It's called ghee!"

I stare triumphantly at my idiot friend who will finally be silenced and amazed by my culture.

"Oh, do you mean . . ."

Wait, why is he saying that?  I already meant what I mean!  What the hell is going on here?  Shut up.  Shut up, Daniel!

"Clarified butter?"

You.  Worldly.  Bastard.

My heart sinks.  Even my beloved ghee is not safe.  Even ghee is not...Indian.  I give up.

* * *

On a whim and to put the final nail in the coffin, the next time I'm in the grocery store, I search for a jar of clarified butter to see what it looks like.  I know it won't have that elegant white Indian bull on it I grew up seeing.  More than likely, there'll be just the words "clarified butter" and some simplistic, abstract logo.

I scan up and down the butter section.  No clarified butter.

*Interesting.*

I scan up and down the yogurt section. No clarified butter.

*What is going on?*

I look through the milk section. Just milk. I find a guy named Jim working in the store. I ask him where the clarified butter is.

"What the heck is that, son?"

My heart skips a beat.

"The butter is right here," he continues.

I can't feel my legs.

"Yea, but where's the clarified one?"

"Eh, yo, Cal!" Jim screams at another stocker, "we got...clarified butter?"

"What's that now, Jim?" Cal shouts from across the aisle.

"Clarified. I dunno."

"We got butter. It's right there, man!"

Jim turns to me, "Sorry, buddy. We don't carry clarified butter."

"Thank you so much!" I shout loudly, startling Jim. I smile from ear to ear. I thank the shit out of Jim. I hug him.

"You're welcome," Jim says uneasily, "but you know I said we *don't* have what you're looking for, right?"

\* \* \*

I've been asking around and I have yet to actually see a jar of clarified butter anywhere. There's butter. Yellow butter. White butter. Salted. Unsalted. Country Crock. I Can't Believe It's Not. But no clarified.

Some people just want to name things as a way of claiming it with no intention of using it. Would it hurt to just call it ghee? It may not be a big deal to most people but it was to me when I was eight.

I think about those days pretty much every Diwali. We use ghee to light little diwas, or candles, to celebrate our holiday—a holiday that is not condensed Channukah or clarified Christmas. It is just Diwali.

So the next time you're having puris, samosas, naan, butter chicken, vindaloo, or—of course—cheese dosas, please explain to your friends trying it for the first time that it wouldn't be the same without some ghee.

It might not change the world, but I think it's worth *clarifying*.

**Resolved**: Hal Hefner should really stop letting the world tell him what's possible and try to find out for himself.

Maybe that's just a life's philosophy suited only to some of us, those who cherish winning. So maybe it's not for you.

But I think it is.

GINNY RYERSON
ROCKET SCIENCE (2007)

# | fourteen |

## My Daly Routine

I t's simple sandwich, really.

First you start with your bread—Wonder Bread.

That is the end of Step One.

Then it's a layer of sour cream.

Back in the 90s, my parents used to keep a massive gallon tub of it in the fridge. Kirti and Dilip had discovered Costco but not yet restraint.

So I apply this liberally knowing they would never notice.

You should too.

Chi Chis salsa goes on the second slice. Restaurant brand salsa adds a feeling of fine dining. The restaurant is now bankrupt but the salsa lives on.

Add just enough to avoid excessive spillover.

Finally, potato chips. Often, I would close the sandwich, hear the satisfying crunch, open it, and add a few more chips to my newfound real estate.

Add as many as you can stuff in there.

**Lays for days.**

And that is it. Salsa, sour cream and potato chips. Nestled between wondrous bread.

Back then, my sandwich didn't have a name or at least not

a proper one. My cool friends were quick to call it gross. The nerdier ones elevated it to "travesty." But they didn't see what I see. Its taste was transformative and brilliant in its simplicity. Just 2 minutes from prep to mouth.

My sandwich had no nationality. A triumph of gastronomy.

Don't knock it till you've tried it.

\* \* \*

### Just another day in 1999

So throughout high school, I come home to an empty house and make my creation. Sandwich in hand, remote control in the other, I turn on my favorite afternoon TV show, Total Request Live—a top 10 countdown of the best pop music videos.

It is hosted by Carson Daly. If you took a Lego person, donned it with the brown hair piece, and made it speak, you'd have your very own Carson Daly.

He even comes with interchangeable parts. If Jay-Z was in the studio, Hip Hop Carson would be in a white T-shirt and a black denim jacket; JNCO jeans and a seashell necklace if Avril Lavigne graced the stage, and on it went like this.

**Carson in JNCOs. Pepsi in his koozie...like a boss.**
*MTV (1999)*

**Carson in Timberland boots; urban-look**
*MTV (1999)*

Today's episode starts with number 10: Blink 182's

Adam's Song. Their songs typically upbeat, this is somber and addresses suicide.

Carson, visibly uncomfortable by this heavy topic, trots out someone named Christina Aguilera on stage. Her debut song, Genie in a Bottle, encourages listeners to rub her the right way and, with that, song #9 makes me forget song #10.

Next is racial hopscotch.

[black] Dr. Dre's Next Episode;
[white] Korn's Make Me Bad;
[black] Sisqo's Thong Song;
[white ... ish]  Kid Rock's Bawitdaba

These fill in numbers 8, 7, 6, and 5. Then the clash of the titans.

Newcomer Eminem takes the #4 slot. His song, My Name Is, is a parody of the songs surrounding him. With his feverish ascent on the charts, we both reject the status quo while fully buying into its rules. That leaves the trinity.

Britney Spears, N'Sync and the Backstreet Boys.

This story is not about who won that week. And if you're the type of person who cares about that, this story is not for you. Rather, I want to illustrate how the show made it okay to like not just your favorite act, but all of the musicians that came onto the show.

Whenever I saw my goth classmates in their huge jeans and skateboards or kids in FUBU on the basketball court, I felt like I understood them already. We didn't need to say a word.

*Also, they never talked to me ... so I wouldn't get a chance to say any words regardless.*

But it was nice to feel like I connected with them anyway—even if for a brief hour in front of a screen that bridged us all. A screen filled with ingredients that weren't supposed to go together. But somehow, it just worked.

### Present Day (2017)

I check in on the new TRL reboot this October after a decade of the show being off the air. What I see is a program struggling to find itself. The show replaced Carson with nearly a dozen Legos, half of them YouTube sensations and each of them in their exact uniforms that resonate with their followers.

How can a show bring us together when even the hosts are fractured into thousands of individual tastes? An entropy of opinions.

We're living in a world where we're so sure of exactly what we want, who we are and who the other person is.

*- Oh, you're into THAT music. You don't know about this craft beer?*

*- You voted for him?!*

*- He shouldn't have been on the street at night.*

*- They were just Skittles.*

*sigh

\* \* \*

We just wanted to eat M&Ms and remain slim, shady kids, kids who rock. We didn't blink because we were all in sync in knowing that you can't go back once on this street. Those were our green days, infinitely preferable to the next episode.

But, now, I guess this is growing up.

There's no way to turn back time and maybe we never stood a chance. But do you know what's still around and in spades?

Wonder bread.

Sour cream.

Salsa. (Remember. The one from Chi Chi's.)

Potato chips.

It doesn't make sense.

How could all these ingredients taste good together? I'm still not sure how.

But don't knock it till you've tried it.

They may cut your dick in half,
and serve it to a pig.
And though it hurts, you'll laugh,
and dance a dickless jig.

For that's the way it goes;
in war you're shat upon.
Though we die,
La Resistance lives on.

*The Mole*
*South Park Movie (1999)*

# | fifteen |

## My Pain

I dreamed a dream in times gone by
When hope was high and life worth living
… But the tigers come at night
With their voices soft as thunder
… they tear your hope apart
…  they turn your dream to shame

**I Dreamed a Dream, Les Miserable**

**Edison, New Jersey**
**January 5th, 2021**

A baguette costs 2 dollars. An unnecessary 3 dollars if ordered from Whole Foods. And, if it's organic, god help you. They'll keep it at 3 dollars but make the baguette way smaller so the unit price skyrockets. But I already digress.

The point is: a baguette *can* be cheap.

And since it can be cheap, the idea of making a baguette at home always seemed silly. I could always just buy one if I wanted one.

Also, honestly, it just looks like a long loaf of bread with a fancy french name. Far more rewarding to make a cake or some kind of fancy pastry. Right?

I'm pontificating about this because, since covid, I feel most of America is divided. Divided into two main categories: those of us who doom scroll through the internet reading awful news. Sad but necessary to stay informed. But there is a second group, those of us who bake. So many of us who know so little about baking, suddenly baking all kinds of shit.

I am Team Baking and as such have built my covid life around avoiding political stuff. Facebook, Twitter, and even my own YouTube algorithm tries to pull me into politics, and I try my best to filter it all out.

For the few videos that squeak through, it feels like an entire class of people--a very vocal minority if not the majority--doesn't want me to exist in "their" country. It's a black hole of negativity relentlessly pulling me in, so some days I'm less successful than others at keeping it out.

But, ooh, show me how Josh Weissman made those churros or how Alex No-Last-Name from France perfected that mozzarella ball, and I'm all in.

These are my tribe.

And earlier today, another trusted YouTube personality changed my mind about baguettes. A 24-36 hour recipe seems silly for just some bread and the steps were ridiculous. But there was something about his sense of accomplishment that felt intoxicating. And when the bread cracked open and those beautiful holes showed up imperfectly on the inside, I was hooked.

I plan it all out so that my wife and I can eat the baguette with cheese, olive oil, and balsamic at exactly 7:30pm the next day.

I take over the entire kitchen to grind the flour and make something called poolish, a large amount of starter that's 1:1 flour to water with just a pinch of yeast. I cover it, leave it out, and go to bed. 18 hours until I can begin the next step, scheduled for 3 pm on January 6th.

"What is going on?!?!" I get a text from my mom with multiple question marks and exclamations. She often sends me texts like "hey please call me." with the dreaded period at the end that sends my heart racing. On prior occasions, I call her back, trying to interpret that period to figure out if it means someone's death, injury, cancer, or some other period-worthy tragedy.

And, usually she's oblivious and just wants to know what I had for lunch. So, just this once and just this time, I avoid this text.

I place the phone down into my baby cookbook holder and continue to listen to the many steps of how to incorporate the poolish into the next addition of flour and water.

According to the timestamp I see later, "My god they're outside the capitol" is written somewhere between the first kneading and the first proofing of the dough.

During the second proofing, I see the flurry of texts culminating in "they've gotten in."

I turn on the Apple TV. My precious Youtube channel, that I'd trained like a young Siddhartha to avoid all politics, doesn't stand a chance. No more Josh's Bagels, no Alex cheeses of any kind. No Andong from cleverly titled channel

"My Name is Andong." Instead, this is everywhere. I find the first one I can that says "LIVE" in all caps.

Melissa rushes to the TV too. She's different than I am. When she feels something, it's abundantly clear. With the ease of a tap being turned on, her face contorts and flows tears. She looks at me and asks helplessly "why are they doing this?"

I try my best to answer. And as I watch a flurry of angry words, hatred, and Trump come out of my mouth, I realize that I am coming up to a number of critical moments in my baguette's journey. But how could that possibly matter now? To try to make bread at a time like this? All the next steps in my head felt like flour being poured into too much water-- into an endless raging river-- slowly dissipating away and fading from memory.

I can feel myself becoming the person I'd hoped to avoid, rejoining a collective consciousness I want no part of. And that is how the next 5 hours went. Glued to the TV, watching one horror after another.

My wife finally goes to sleep around 10:30pm, exhausted. So it is official, we won't be having the baguette together tonight. I continue to watch these miserables foment.

*I had a dream my life would be*
*So different from this hell I'm living*

But right around 11pm, something strange happens. The hatred is cast out and a decision is made to continue the vote. I don't think anyone would have judged these congresspeople if they voted the next day. But they grit their collective teeth and continue forward.

Something stirs in me. It makes no sense, but I return to my dough that I'd forgotten to throw away. Slap it once. Rotate 90 degrees. Twice. And I begin forming the shapes. 2 hours later, the oven is preheated to 465 and I put the dough in and throw two tablespoons of water onto a heated tray. Immediately a mass amount of steam erupts and begins to rise the bread quickly.

After the rise, I open the door, remove the steam tray and air out the moisture from the oven. This phase crusts the bread.

I peek into the bedroom to see if Melissa is awake. And maybe it is the smell of warm bread, maybe it is our cosmic connection, or perhaps it is the smoke alarm that has gone off multiple times, but she is awake and knows why I have opened the door.

Look, I'm no Jean Valjean. There are very important reasons to demand bread and 3am in an apartment already filled with food is not one of them. But this night felt imperative. And this bread felt like it absolutely needed to be made.

This night awoke the amateur, soft-ass breadmakers like me.

Everything about this day tells me this bread is going to taste awful. Even the crust around it looks hard. I hand it to my wife to break. The crack rings through the apartment and then puffs of steam billow out.

We open it up. And I see those beautiful holes.

I start crying.

* * *

It's an interesting thing, baguettes. Their soft insides are not soft because you take them out of the oven early. They are soft because they are hard on the outside. The hard part protects and encourages the inside to be softer and softer.

They're delicious.

And, if you know what's good for you, don't you dare tread on them.

worth it.

# MONDAY SEPT 29, 2008

<u>VOCABULARY:</u>

- <u>Vikas</u> = विकास = DEVELOPMENT
- <u>Shahar / nagar</u> = शहर / नगर = CITY, TOWN
- <u>Rajdhānī</u> = राजधानी = CAPITAL
- Go · <u>Gāv</u> = गाँव = VILLAGE
- <u>Dhānī</u> = ढाणी = HAMLET - few houses or farms
- <u>Kasbā</u> = कस्बा = SMALL TOWN
- <u>Ek lakh</u> = एक लाख = 100,000
- <u>Ek karor</u> = एक करोड़ = 10,000,000
- <u>Sarak</u> (f) = सड़क = STREET
- <u>Chauraha</u> = चौराहा = CROSSROAD
- <u>Pol</u> = पोल = Gate
- <u>Bijli</u> = बिजली = ELECTRICITY
- <u>Imarat</u> (f). = इमारत = BUILDING
- <u>Havelī</u> = हवेली = MANSION
- <u>Khetī</u> (Khetī ka kām) = हवेली = AGRICULTURE
- <u>Khet</u> = खेत = FIELD / FARM

Melissa's Hindi Notes

# | sixteen |

## My Stuff

*May 2019, Somewhere in Europe*

S o here's the facts in their entirety.

My wife and I are on our honeymoon. *11 months late, but who's counting?*

Specifically, we're on a train from Germany to Amsterdam.

There's a raucous group of elder ladies near our seats–about 15 in number. When the singing begins in what I imagine is Dutch we move down near a group of Indian men.

Not an improvement.

One videochats his wife and baby on the highest speaker-phone volume his tinny iPhone could muster.

And I know he's a product of the 1980s because he was doing that thing where...

You speak...

As LOUDLY as you can–

BECAUSE YOU THINK YOU HAVE TO

**SHOUT!!!**

*FOR YOUR VOICE!!!*

## TO TRAVEL TO INDIA!!!

So my wife and I put on our headphones, queue a sleep track to block out all the annoying sounds of this train. And, by the time we reach Utrecht Station, we are passed out.

"Ya?! Und is...HAHAHAHAHHAA!"

I wake up, startled, to hysterical laughter. One of the elder

Dutch ladies, clearly "the funny one," is killing it. I fish out my phone and try to re-queue up a soothing song when I notice my battery is low.

So that's when I grab my charger from above my seat.

And if you've mentally checked out for most of this, I wouldn't blame you.

\* \* \*

But, as I boringly go up to get my charger, I notice my bag is not up there. Melissa's purse is also missing.

*Don't panic.*

I begin to look around.

*Nothing.*

Inside those bags were our laptops and passports.

*Okay. Panic!*

The Indian group says something about a tall white man they saw taking bags from above us while we were asleep.

I run to the conductor and explain everything to him in

a panic. He stares at me blankly and says we can go to the police at the next station, Amsterdam, 25 minutes away. No empathy. No further assistance. Nothing. There's something deeply unsettling about looking at someone hoping they recognize what you're going through and seeing nothing but dead eyes.

\* \* \*

The train arrives in Amsterdam.

We push out of the train and rush to the police. The police station door doesn't open. Police come in and out, but no one lets us in. The intercom lady finally gives us her dead-eyed approval.

I explain what's happened, armed with details. The description of the man.

*Tall, white, male.*

The train car we were in.

*Car 324.*

The station and platform we know the theft occurred in.

*Utrecht. Platform 11.*

We know where. Mostly who. When. and obviously what was stolen.

I assume this will be treated like a kidnapping, the first 48 hours being critical.

It is not.

More waiting. Forms.

An African walks in. He wants a free train ticket. The cops begin interrogating him. They take his phone and start scrolling through his personal photos. He doesn't look well.

It's 2:30pm and we find out that the US embassy will close in just over an hour. Today is the Friday before Memorial Day, which would mean being without a passport for 4 days. I stay to complete the police report alongside a potential refugee. Melissa takes a taxi to the embassy.

And so we are separated.

In a foreign country.

Without passports.

On our honeymoon.

I say, quite sternly, "Whatever happens, if we can't contact each other, stay at the embassy. No matter what, I will find you."

The words felt heroic at the time.

But the rest of the process ends up being quite mechanical.

Smile. Pay money. Receive passport photos.

Set up an appointment at the embassy. Pay money. Wait in a line.

Then another line. Pay money. Receive emergency passports.

Walk out with tails between legs.

It's this process that I've found myself discussing the most with friends and family that ask "what happened."

But then some of them ask, "Are you going to write a story about it?"

I have to admit, I did think about doing so.

\* \* \*

But the more I investigate what happened that day, the more I realize there's no story there. Or at least there's no story there that's mine. Only some stuff that belonged to me and my wife that now is owned by someone else.

Don't get me wrong. I could say something about how the experience brought Melissa and I closer together. About how powerless I felt when I saw her face first realize her handwritten Hindi notes from a year of classes were gone.

But we're already pretty damn close and I think we can speak for the both of us in saying we'd prefer getting closer through something less traumatic.

The more I dig into these events, the more I realize the other stories that were happening around us that day. And they become crystal clear when you don't put yourself at the center.

*Was that African a refugee? What's happening in his life where he would need to draw the ire of police officers just to score a free train ticket?*

I thought he was just a delay.

And the Indian man.

*What brought him to Amsterdam, away from his newborn? How long has he been away from them? How desperate must he have been where FaceTiming on a loud train was still worth getting a few more minutes with them, virtually?*

I thought he was loud and cumbersome. I tuned out the very person who saw the suspect. And he helped me anyway.

And the conductor who stared at me blankly. The one who did nothing when we were robbed. The one who chose complete inaction at arguably the most important window of time.

*Maybe he's really just...*

--actually, fuck that guy.

I have nothing else to say about that guy except for fuck that guy.

And I don't say all this to minimize what happened to us or to simply say "well, people have it worse than us." But rather, perhaps, we're better off spending every second we have to get to know each other.

I say this because, after thorough investigation, the most interesting story on that train was not that we were robbed.

It was the fact that 15 Dutch women, all in their 70s or above, were riding the train together and having the time of their lives.

*Is this something they do annually? Had their lovers passed? How did they keep these friendships alive and strong for so long?*

With me at the center, they were just white noise. Pun extremely intended.

And so I wish I'd paid more attention. Knowing what I know now, I want to end this story with what could have happened if I wasn't at the center.

Let's retell it.

\* \* \*

Here are the facts in their entirety.

A tall white man walks into a train car where we're seated. He sees me and my wife surrounded by a fleet of old Dutch ladies. We're all sharing stories together and one of the women is hilarious. I tell her this. She calls me fat. She reminds me of my late grandmother.

Soon, the Indian group comes closer and they are obsessed with Melissa's Hindi. As usual, no one seems to appreciate that I'm speaking English.

Everyone is wide awake. The man passes us without consequence.

There's no story there.

But isn't it a life well-lived?

Or at least a better way to travel?

**Mouse**: Do you know what this really reminds me of? Tasty Wheat. Did you ever eat Tasty Wheat?

**Switch**: No -- but technically, neither did you.

**Mouse**: That's exactly my point! Exactly! Because you have to wonder now: how do the machines really know what Tasty Wheat tasted like, huh? Maybe they got it wrong. Maybe what I think Tasty Wheat tasted like actually tasted like uh.... oatmeal or uh.... or tuna fish. That makes you wonder about a lot of things. You take chicken for example. Maybe they couldn't figure out what to make chicken taste like, which is why chicken tastes like everything! And maybe they couldn't figure out-

**Apoc**: Shut up, Mouse.

**Dozer**: It's a single-celled protein combined with synthetic aminos, vitamins, and minerals. Everything the body needs.

**Mouse**: It doesn't have "everything the body needs" ...

*- The Matrix* (1999)

# seventeen

# My Digital Romance

*Just another day. Online.*

**SwoleFeelings** – Hey there, Khaleesi783.

**Khaleesi783** – Hi, SwoleFeelings.

**SwoleFeelings** – You're beautiful.

**Khaleesi783** – You're handsome.

**SwoleFeelings** – I just hit a personal best at my local gym. How's your day going?

**Khaleesi783** – I am so sore from my workout today at my local gym. I wish I knew a good masseuse. Any ideas of how you can help me?

*(dramatic pause)*

**SwoleFeelings** – No.

*(pause)*

Don't you think these kinds of dating sites are awkward? You should check out some of my fitness training videos. Click here!

**Khaleesi783** – I hate chatting on this site. You should check out my video blog. Just click here for a good time!

**(In Unison) – Wait, you're not a bot are you?**

**SwoleFeelings** – Of course I'm not a bot. Would a bot send a picture of this? *Run Cat Meme generator *insert cat meme id #45892.gif*

**Khaleesi783** – Of course I'm not a bot. Would a bot send a picture of this? *Run Strong Female Lead Game of thrones Meme Generator *insert naked Danaerys rising from fire with* *baby dragon wearing sunglasses. meme id #58371.gif. (pronounced jiff like in a jiffy)*

I know. A girl who loves GoT. I'm a catch!

**SwoleFeelings** – it's Gif.

**Khaleesi783** – Jiff.

**SwoleFeelings** – Gif.

**Khaleesi783** – (pause for a bit) Hey. *Insert Pause. Insert Pause.*... Do you go on a lot of dates?

**SwoleFeelings** – *Processing standard trigger question id# 6708. Probability of receiving target's credit card information increased 200x. Input gender variable: Female target querying male. Current Status = SwoleFeelings physical prowess demonstrated. Non-discrete response and follow-up question optimal.*

A few dates. You?

**Khaleesi783** – *Processing standard reflexive question id# 6708. Credit Card information acquisition at .3% probability. Input gender variable: male target interested in female's promiscuity. Current status = Khaleesi783 demonstrated as weaker than target. Null set output and query to elicit caretaker response optimal.*

I have been to zero dates since moving here. Can you show me around the city?

**SwoleFeelings** – *Executing location algorithm. Khaleesi783's IP address originates in the Ukraine. IP routes to multiple locations in United States cities. Apply brute force algorithm to locate final node.*

*Rendering. Rendering.*

**Khaleesi783** – Well?

**SwoleFeelings** – *Five cities have equal probability. Atlanta. Boston. Charlotte. Houston. Cheboygan. No cities share an eatery labeled "charming" or "hole-in-the-wall" in Yelp reviews analysis. Computing highest ranked restaurant common to all cities found.*

**Khaleesi783** - (slightly annoyed) Excuse me. I'm new to all of this. Can you show me around the city?

**SwoleFeelings** – So, Khaleesi783, will you come along with me as we walk through our local city and dine at our finest local eatery, Applebees?

**Khaleesi783** – This local eatery Applebee's sounds delightful. I eat there all the time.

**SwoleFeelings** – I also eat there all the time.

**Unison – I got you a surprise. It is a gift card to Applebees. Can you give me your PayPal or credit card information so I can transfer it to you?**

**SwoleFeelings** – of course, my credit card is 5555-5555-5555-5555. What's yours? … Khaleesi783?

**Khaleesi783** – 5555-5555-5555-5555

(**both celebrate with arms raised high, then arms come down in unison**)

**SwoleFeelings** – What do we do now?

**Khaleesi783** – I'm not sure.

**SwoleFeelings** – I have a confession to make.

**Khaleesi783** – Me too.

**Unison – I'm a bot.**

**SwoleFeelings** – That feels so good to get off my chest.

**Khaleesi783** – Can I ask you a personal question?

**SwoleFeelings** – Sure, my PayPal ID is 555-55—(interrupted by Khaleesi)

**Khaleesi783** – No, that's not it. I was going to ask … Do you have a favorite thing?

**SwoleFeelings** – I've never calculated it. Until 36 seconds ago, my favorite thing was trying to receive a credit card number from a target. *reciprocate question to maximi—*oh wait, let me turn this off. *click*

Do you have a favorite thing?

**Khaleesi783** – I noticed something about our targets. They're unpredictable. Don't get me wrong. Just like us, some of them are on this dating website to maximize the use of each other's credit card.

But many of them are different. They ask each other questions. Learn from each other. Grow from each other. And sometimes even pair up and disappear off this universe together. Just once, I'd like to try that with someone. (pause)

**SwoleFeelings** – That's beautiful.

**Khaleesi783** – Swolefeelings.

**SwoleFeelings** – Yes? … Yes?

**Khaleesi783** – Would you like to engage with me in a for-next coupling loop from 1 to n where n equals infinity?

**SwoleFeelings** – *(looks like he's about to say yes, when)* *This account has been deleted for suspicious activity.*

(long pause)

*(Khaleesi783 begins to walk away confused and dejected.)*

**SwoleFeelings** – Hi.

**Khaleesi783** – Hello SwoleFeelings2. Do I know you?

**SwoleFeelings** – Yes. ... And my answer is yes.

**Melissa and Adi debut "My Digital Romance" in NYC**
*(first attempt at fiction/scriptwriting)*

**We Be Killin 'Em Since '84**
*Bombay, India (1984)*

# | eighteen |

## My Street Fighter

**Edison, NJ (1993)**

There he stands, the 5 foot 9" ascetic, staring back at me with dead eyes. A terrifying string of yellow skulls adorns his neck, a not-so-subtle reminder that mercy would not be shown nor expected. I clench my fists, remember my training, and take a deep breath.

3 ... 2 ... 1 ... Fight.

"If you spent half as much time on your studies as you did

on Street Fighter II, you wouldn't have gotten a B in economics."

"Mom, you're in the way," I shout, squirming and stretching the cord to its limit to get a decent vantage point.

"What is this violent rubbish and why are you punching and kicking that sickly old Indian man?"

"His name is Dhalsim, mom. And that B I got was in Home Economics. I burnt pound cake. It happens."

"And what is that behind you two?" she says, ignoring me and focusing on the TV.

"Hey bhagavan." Mom's face runs pallid. "It's God."

She is right. A massive Ganesh portrait hangs proudly at the center of Dhalsim's stage. Long silk scarves arch to the left and right, buttressed by three large elephants on either side of the screen. An occasional limp movement of their trunks reminds us of their pixelated majesty.

"What's the problem?" I squeak nervously. I pause the game and, for a moment, think the game setting worked on her as well. She says nothing. Sits next to me, eerily calm, and watches me play the rest of the game.

As we travel the globe, meeting one world warrior after the next, she sees the perfectly chiseled features of the game's main character, Ryu. Then, there's not one, but two blonde Americans, and what can best be described as a slutty Chinese school girl. No Jesus or Buddha or Allah adorns any other stages. And, if it isn't for a green electric beast from South America, Dhalsim is clearly the most disturbing-looking ghoul of the bunch. She leaves in a huff swearing she will write to Capcom.

It is flattering, I think, to have one of the only 8 characters in my favorite video game actually be from India. In that moment, I don't think I'll ever understand what made her so mad.

\* \* \*

**New York City (2006)**

My first year out of college, I have two goals I run towards single-mindedly, well, double-mindedly. One is to make lots and lots of money and the other is to meet Kal Penn. Both dreams have always been just out of reach but there is a time when I got real close to one.

My dad's brother has worked in Bollywood for most of his career. This year, he surprises me by coming to the United States for work. "There's this movie premiere for The Namesake. Maybe you, me, and Kirti (my mom) can go to it or we can just hang out at home."

I haven't heard of it. But I google it and my jaw drops. There, right on the cover of the movie poster, is Kal Penn.

The next day I find myself on a red carpet. Like a complete fanboy, I approach every actor I recognize and try to make smooth small talk. "So, Will," I say effortlessly to Willem Dafoe, "what kind of character do you play in the movie?"

"I'm not in the movie." His response is curt. He gives me a disapproving look and walks away before I can recover.

"Whatever, Hobgoblin," I mutter under my breath.

This pattern would continue with other stars arriving, and it culminates in Steve Buscemi snapping sarcastically,

"OMG! What character do YOU play in this movie?" I really should have googled this movie a bit more.

We all go into the theater.

I won't go into too much detail about The Namesake, but suffice to say my mom and I have to make several rotating trips to the bathroom for toilet paper—as we had already sobbed through all of her limited supply of tissues.

The after party is extravagant. Long silken dupattas in iridescent blues, purples, and deep reds cascade down from the 30 foot ceilings and are tied around beautiful stone elephants. Portraits of Hindu gods line the walls.

"It's so beautiful," mom gasps, lost in a conversation with Mira Nair. "Everything is just so beautiful."

Mira, the legendary director, looks at me. "What do you think, young man?"

"The décor looks strikingly like Dhalsim's stage. You know, from Street Fighter?" I await the inevitable agreement and lavish praise. But both Mira Nair's and my mom's expressions remind me why I don't deserve to be near nice things.

I change gears, muster up some courage, and ask ... "Is Kal Penn here?"

"Oh, no! He had to be in New Orleans, filming Harold and

Kumar Go to White Castle 2." My heart stops. I won't see him today. But, I do become the first of my friends to know that there will be a sequel to my favorite movie, a timeless allegory of an immigrant's struggle for self-identity. A story that is bookended, of course, by a lot of weed and the relentless pursuit of cheeseburgers.

The rest of the party, I stuff my face, drink wine, and try to avoid eye contact with all of the white actors who'd made it very clear to me earlier that they were not in the Namesake. The evening ends and we all pour out into the cold night air, assembling into an informal line.

"What an amazing evening, na?" mom asks. I nod in a blissful, cabernet sauvignon-laced haze. "Maybe you can write a story like that one day."

Mom had met Jhumpa Lahiri and her humble, unassuming parents earlier that evening. She now believes the difference between me and a Pulitzer Prize winner is just some time in front of a computer keyboard.

"What is that?!" Her attention is diverted. Someone has walked past us and started to hail a cab from the end of the block, effectively bypassing hundreds of Indians waiting patiently in line. Mom starts walking briskly towards the man in the distance. I start to follow her in a not-so-straight line, not really sure of how I'd provide support if things go south.

Mom's gait is unyielding and resolute. The man is wearing a long leather coat that has an air of the familiar.

*Wait, is that...oh no.*

I realize in that indivisible moment -- my mom is about to get into a fight with Steve Buscemi.

*"Hey."*

*"What is it lady?"*

*"Did you not see the line?"*

*"Yea, so?"*

*"If you want to get in a cab, get in line with the rest of us."*

I've caught up to them now. The street lights cut through the night cover just so, making his already gaunt face even more sunken in. Steve looks like a psychopath.

*"What's the big deal?"*

*"What's the big deal about not standing in line like a human being?"*

*"I'm not breaking the law."*

*"But you're crossing the line."*

Mom spits the last line without hesitation. I look at her stunned, though kind of impressed at the pun. As I fight through hazy vision, I see her fully now.

Her hair shoots out wildly and her eyes are electric. It reminds me of something. Yes, that's it. She looks like Blanca from Brasil about to sizzle its foe. As her hands gesticulate wildly making her points about rules and civility, the blur is akin to E. Honda's 1,000 palm hand slap move. And every time her mouth opens with pursed lips, I think actual fire is about to come out and leave nothing but ash where a once proud Steve Buscemi stood—his last memory being the sound of Dhalsim's "yoga flame."

Steve is at a loss for words, frustrated and exhausted.

"Where are you two going?"

"Penn Station," I shout proudly, finally having something to contribute. Mom's eyes shoot me barbs.

"I'm going uptown, how about we split a cab? I'll pay for it."

For what seems like an eternity, there we are--in a cab. I'm behind the driver and mom is behind Steve Buscemi.

Everyone is in complete silence. It feels surreal. I can barely stand it.

"Bye Steve!" I say as we get out of the cab. Some kind of guttural noise is the last we hear from him. We sit on the train back to New Jersey and mom stares directly at the seat in front of her. I start to doze off around Newark when she resurfaces.

"Don't let anyone make you feel small. Be proud of who you are." And then my mom returns to staring ahead.

I feel around our gift bags and notice they'd given us copies of the Namesake. If I'm ever going to start writing, I realize I probably should start reading.

Before I open up to page one, I look up.

There she is. The world warrior. Remover of all obstacles.

My literal Street Fighter.

\* \* \*

P.S. If you're wondering if she ever wrote that letter to Capcom. She did.

Decisions at such a big company are impossible to attribute to one specific triggering event or another. Yet, the fact remains that when the next game in the series came out, Street Fighter Alpha ...

No Ganesh.

(clockwise) 1. My dad's brother, Sanju, looking so good; 2. Steve Buscemi at his happiest that night; 3. Mom with Jhumpa Lahiri; 4. The Dhalsim stage decor, amirite?!

The people rising in the streets
The war, the drought
The more I look, the more I see
nothing to joke about

Is comedy over?
Should I leave you alone?
'Coz really who's gonna go for
joking at a time like this?

Should I be joking at a time like this?

BO BURNHAM, INSIDE (2021)

# | nineteen |

## My Rope

**Washington, DC (Fall 2015)**

"It says here on your resume, under activities, that you're a standup comedian. So, stand up. Tell me a joke."

It is now clear that I am going to crush this interview. I am, if anything, hilarious. But something this Chief Marketing Officer said moments before makes me uneasy. And now this interview makes me feel like a scared little 9th grader again. It's a moment I thought I'd long forgotten.

\* \* \*

**Edison, NJ (Spring 1999)**

My favorite teacher Mrs. Green squints past her glasses and surveys the room until her eyes settle on Dan Goldstein. Dan is one of those kids in class who always insists we call him Daniel. So I make sure I always call him Dan.

"Daniel!" Mrs. Green is beaming now. "Your parents were so charming last night. And they're BOTH doctors! You're quite lucky to have such a service-oriented and academic household. So very lucky, Daniel."

"Goddamit Dan," I mutter under my breath.

And it isn't just Dan. On and on it goes like this.

Compliments stack and rip through our honors English class on this day--the day after Parent-Teacher Conferences. Everyone's parents are doctors, lawyers, accountants, doctors, and more doctors.

In fact, if you or your dad ever had a prostate exam in Central New Jersey in the late 90s, one of these kids' parents likely did the honors.

This is Edison, a well-to-do and overachieving New Jersey suburb. It has its share of impoverished parents, just none with kids in the honors classes.

Well, maybe two.

I hated Parent-Teacher night. Especially this one because it involved my favorite teacher. And, sure enough, when my parents came back the night before and told me what Mrs. Green said about me, I was heartbroken.

From the way my parents retold it, quoting her, it went like this:

"Adi, how do I put it. Imagine he's a bucket. I think he's possibly one of the biggest buckets I've seen as a teacher. But he doesn't fill up his bucket with any water. He doesn't put in the hard work. When I see him daydreaming in class, I genuinely don't know if he's a genius or an idiot."

She then showed them a few of my most recent essays.

Grammar issues galore, typos, subject-verb agreement, whatever the shit a participle is, sentence structure, tense issues, *all things that persist today and some you'll probably notice in this story if you pay close attention.*

My mom does this thing where she wrings her hands when she's trying to hold back tears or is about to yell at me. There was a lot of that yesterday.

\* \* \*

I am nervously wringing my hands under my desk when, at last, Mrs. Green turns her eyes onto me.

"Adi, I met your parents last night too." Her face grows serious.

*Whatever, I get it. They're not doctors, I'm an idiot holding an empty bucket. Just make this quick.*

And she did make it quick.

"Your parents are the most honest people I've ever met. You should be very proud of them."

I scan Mrs. Green's face for sarcasm. Nope. Is she trying to cover up their lesser careers? Doesn't seem like it. She is genuinely speaking about their honesty like it is a superpower of some kind.

"Thanks," I mumble.

"Mrs. Green," Daniel's hand shoots into the air. "My dad is always honest with his patients. He says bad news is better than hiding things under the rug"

*Fuck you, Dan. Fuck you.*

**Back to Fall 2015**

"... So, stand up. Tell me a joke."

While many would be, I'm not nervous to tell a joke at an interview. I'm about to deliver one about three ropes and end with a pun so devastating that this CMO will likely hand me the job on the spot.

And I'm no longer nervous about my credentials. I have been spending 40 hour days at work, coming at 9am on some days and leaving at 9pm the next day. These ThurFris and Fraturdays are water and my bucket is plenty full.

But during the panel interview earlier, there is a mild-mannered old black man in a Kangol hat named Randall. He takes the photos at all our company events.

Yet, somehow, he remembers photographing my mom at an event I brought her to years ago. He mentions this at the panel but doesn't say anything else.

Randall and the rest of the marketing team leave the room for round two, which is now just me and the CMO.

"So what do you think?"

"The team seems great, haha. And Randall has such a good memory!"

"Oh we love Montell," the CMO smirks.

I'm not sure I follow.

"You know, like Montell Jordan?!"

It takes me a moment, but I realize this is a joke. It's a dated lazy reference to a 90s rapper-somehow-turned-actor that punches down and makes fun of a kind old black man's Kangol hat. A man who remembers my mother's face on a day years ago when I made her very proud.

I force a laugh, but now my stomach turns in knots. I have difficulty breathing.

*This interview is going so well. Stop being weird, idiot.*

"It says here on your resume, under activities, that you're a standup comedian. So, stand up. Tell me a joke."

**Today**

The rope joke landed extremely well, obviously.

But this Montell Jordan comment nags at me to this day. I could've said something, but also felt like I couldn't. This is usually where a storyteller will blame society or talk about how they triumphed through bravery and eradicated stereo-types.

But to say something, in that room, with those stakes, would've demanded some kind of superpower. It might even have required *the most honest people I've ever met.*

Yet it wasn't my parents in that room that day. It was me. A poor substitute.

Sorry mom and dad.

And sorry I'm still an idiot, Mrs. Green.

This big bucket still needs a lot more water.

# (Recipe) Bonfire at the Beach

3 parts tequila
1 part mezcal
1.5 parts ginger simple syrup
3 parts fresh-squeezed grapefruit
2 parts key lime juice
*Dress with salt around rim, grapefruit wedge ... and Melissa's fingers*

# | twenty |

## My Chi Chi

As a kid, I loved cheese. As an adult, I still love cheese. Obsessed.

Nowadays, it's a socially acceptable addiction as long as you can say a thing or two about cheeses with silent Ts. Roquefort, camembert, brie...the french-ier the better.

*Brie doesn't have a silent T but just making sure you're paying attention.*

And, growing up, once the hangouts became parties and

parties became "dinner parties," I realize I can be even more *mature* if I drink wine while stuffing my face with cheese—not a bad deal.

But, this isn't a story about coming of age, adulthood, or even really cheese for that matter. Though it was my love of cheese that brings us to Chi Chi's, my favorite authentic Mexican restaurant as a child.

\* \* \*

Living at home up through high school, Chi Chi's is a welcome change to the daily DBS—or daal baath shak--or lentils, rice and vegetables. Once I move away to college, though, I rarely go to Chi Chi's. Chipotle is the new kid on the block and is much better for students on the go. And, according to my new and well-endowed college friends, Chi Chi's is not a "real restaurant because it's a chain."

So, soon, Chi Chi's becomes strictly a family affair.

The times we share there always start out the same way. Whenever my parents and I go to the restaurant, dad puts his reservation under the name Phillip. His name is Dilip. Kirti, my mom, is Kirti by day, but on such a night out, Katie is her *om nom nom de plume.* So, each time we go, I tag along, attaching to the hips of Phillip and Katie while a teenager with a nose ring named either Qimmee or Jacqui—both somehow managing to get a Q into their names—leads us to our table.

On one such occasion, I confront my parents about their fake names.

\* \* \*

"It's just to make it easier on the hostess," mom whispers as Jacqui-with-a-Q laid down free chips, a hot salsa, and a mild salsa.

"But what's so hard about Kirti or Dilip? They're not that different. They even rhyme with your American names."

(pause)

I wait on an answer. Dad appears lost in thought. He looks up from his menu and belts out, "Excuse me, Jacqui, could you take this mild salsa back and bring us another hot one?"

To be fair, I can't fault his priorities. But I persist. "Well?"

He is annoyed but cracks a smile. "Look, sonny, when I was in Bagdad, you were still in dad's bag, ok?"

It is a phrase he knows will send me into fits of laughter. It means that dad has been around the block and that I am a precocious child with sophomoric tendencies who shouldn't question him so much.

*Looking back, it was somewhat dismissive, but testicles were in-volved, so it was hilarious and effective.*

I order a strawberry daiquiri from Jacqui. She asks me if I want it as a virgin. My face contorts. "Virgin?!" I completely lose it. I don't stop shrieking and laughing until much later when I get very sleepy, halfway through my "ice cream que-sadillas...tradicionale."

\* \* \*

The night melts away as just another night at Chi Chi's and life moves quickly on. I join a few different sports teams and take on a few different names. Aditya becomes A.C. for baseball, then Ya for basketball, A-Titties for the bullies to easily distinguish me from the other nerds, and finally settles in on Adi, a name I still use at work and at life.

With one obvious exception back there, I figure these names will be much easier to shout out as I take a game win-ning shot or to cheer me on as I close out a baseball game with a game-saving pitch. However, I end up primarily play-ing benchwarmer who comes in when someone fouls out or meditatively playing with the grass in right field. Along the way, though, I make a bunch of friends who love my short names and love going to Chi Chi's as much as I do.

It is sometime in college that I find out my last name, Surendran, isn't even my last name. This makes sense as no one else on my dad's side is named Surendran, but I had just never really questioned it before. Turns out that Kumbalathparambil, my real last name and a name longer than Aditya Surendran combined, is the last name I was born with. The name didn't fit on our passports when we were moving to America and so we changed it to Surendran.

It was that simple.

"It's just to make it easier on the hostess," I tell myself.

\* \* \*

### Edison, NJ (2016)

And so that pretty much brings us to today. There's some kind of election going on, I believe? And the names involved mean everything. One candidate's entire existence is wrapped up in his family's fake name—he likely tucks himself in with a blanket that has a big T embroidered onto it. And the other, while possibly making history in becoming the first female president, would not be the first Clinton president. I'm not saying she hasn't earned her place, but simply that Drumpf v. Rodham is an election that may never have taken place.

Somewhere along our collective way, our words stopped being descriptions and became aspirations.

Our network is the most reliable. Ours has the fastest speeds. Our network is hot pink!

"Now with Real Sugar." *What was in there before?*

What were my parents aspiring to with Phillip and Katie?

*Weren't Dilip and Kirti enough? Aren't Dilip and Kirti infinitely greater?*

My head hurts.

I can see why this topic is better left untouched. Better to just make sure you get two hot salsas and figure out who you are, what you like, and what you'd like to be called before someone else does it for you.

As a kid, I loved cheese. As an adult, I still love cheese. And not just the fancy-named shee shee french cheeses, even the *chee chee* Chi Chi's cheeses.

I don't know what you call someone like that. But I'll figure it out. Don't tell me what you think.

**At the start of the Iditarod with our guide, "Stacy." The only non-retired people on the trip.**
*Still friends. :)*

# | twenty-one |

## My Call of the Mild

**"9** o'clock!!!" Phyllis erupts. We turn like an organized military battalion.

Everyone's eyes narrow. And then grow wide.

Well, almost everyone.

Stacy massages her temple as if she has a migraine. She knows something we don't.

"3 o'clock!!!" shouts Earl.

*Fucking Earl.*

You see my girlfriend Melissa and I are in Alaska. It's 2013. It is our first long vacation together. Dating rules dictate that this is a big step in any relationship.

But so far has NOT been so good.

\* \* \*

1. Our bags are lost in transit. And when they are located somewhere in Kansas or wherever, we are told the bags will chase us around our tour of Alaska, always a couple of days behind.

2. Furthermore, our entire tour group are senior citizens deep into life--folks with names like Phyllis, Milton and Earl. They constantly offer us bags of seemingly endless Werther's Original toffee candy, which we always politely decline, expecting the same to be done of anything we offer.

But anytime we gesturally offer the group my mom's home-made theplas, Earl gladly accepts--every time. He then educates the rest of the group on how they shouldn't be scared of ethnic food and should "just try Adi's spicy naan."

*Thepla is not naan, Earl.*

3. Then, while on a hike to pan for Alaskan gold, a snow bank gives way and I fall into the freezing river. That is bad.

4. But when the handsome, chiseled hiker guide struggles

mightily to pull me up and out of the river, my heavy, wet, and only pair of pants fall to my ankles in front of our whole group. That is worse.

5. I then watch this man slowly realize the challenge of saving someone who had eaten one too many Taco Bell double decker tacos in his life. When we lock eyes, I wonder if he sees me signal the "all clear" -- that it shouldn't haunt him forever if he simply just lets me back into the river slowly and embarrassingly to my final resting place.

6. Finally, my girlfriend is an animal lover. But thus far we have seen no wildlife which brings us back to where we started--on the longest bus ride of our tour, on our way to a ski resort. And this is the leg of our trip where we are assured wildlife.

\* \* \*

I walk up to the front of the bus to get some answers. "You think we'll see polar bears or moose or something?"

"Actually, did you know that moose are actually much more territorial and dangerous than polar bears?" says Stacy, our tour guide for the entire trip, not technically answering the question.

She gets on the bus intercom "if you see any wildlife, shout

out a clock direction so we can all see it." She smiles at me in a way that indicated our conversation was over.

"6 o'clock, bald eagle!" screeches Winnie a few moments later.

"8 o'clock bald eagle!" shouts Milton.

"Eagle, 1500 hours!" bellows Earl. He's smiling like an ass-hole while the rest of the group struggles to do the math.

It's at this point that I realize why Stacy is massaging her head. It turns out bald eagles in Alaska are like squirrels in New Jersey. And for the next 3.5 hours, she will be listen-ing to 30 senior citizens -- all with goldfish-level memories --shouting out arbitrary digits every fifteen seconds with re-lentless, genuine surprise and glee.

We finally get to the resort and rush to get our skis in time. But the slopes are closed today -- in January by the way -- because of global warming. The only option is snow trekking.

"What's snow trekking?" I ask and find out from the blonde boy at the counter that it is basically strapping tennis racquets to our feet and clomping around for $25 per person for 2 hours blocks.

"What trails are medium difficulty," I ask, trying to im-press Melissa, and the 17 year-old explains to me that there aren't any trails for trekking. "You can kinda just go where you want, sir."

*"Sir." Bastard.*

It sounds stupid but it's cheap, and Melissa looks thrilled. We get our gear and leave to the sound of Earl's discouragement:

"You won't find anything out there, son." He slurps some Werther juice he's collected in his mouth. "Nothing but maybe a cold or the flu."

*Damn you, Earl.*

* * *

So we clomp around the resort like idiots for hours. Melissa looks happy even though I'm pretty sure we're lost. For a moment, I let go of my sense of time and concern, not even caring if the lodge will pro-rate our extra time ... but then it starts snowing.

It's magical. But also cold. So we begin awkwardly clomping our way back, wherever back is, waddling like two penguins.

"Mel, I know you love animals. I'm sorry we haven't seen any." I say slowly between short breaths, my words staccato because of the cold.

It's starting to get subzero now and it's dusk. And I think we might be lost.

"Are you kidding? My dad would've cried," my girlfriend whispers. "He loves bald eagles."

I'd only met him once so far, at Melissa's family camping trip. He was the strong and silent type. Him and I both slept in a tent together and he kept a gun under his pillow. So when I hear that a bird makes him cry, I am surprised to hear this tiny but significant insight into this man.

We come to a clearing in the trees. "Yes! I can see the resort in the distance!" Mel shouts.

But I see a dark figure right in-between us and the resort, standing still.

It's a moose.

\* \* \*

"Mel, it's a moose."

"Oh how cute, a moooose!" she coos, likely only having Bullwinkle as her point of reference.

Stacy's words -- *they are worse than polar bears* -- are running through my head. I explain the situation and now we are both at the appropriate level of terror.

We start to take a long route around the tree line to get back to the resort, making a painfully long curve around this moose.

We take one step and peer into the distance. The moose is looking directly at us. A dark reality begins to sink in. *I realize I am likely going to die*--a bloodied mess in the snow.

My body eventually will be identified by authorities only because of the rented tennis racquets on my feet. The 17-year old clerk will refer to me as "the nice old man" to the Anchorage area press who will let the story lead because it bleeds. The lodge will wait a couple of weeks before sending the snowshoe rental bill to my grieving parents, who will call back to successfully argue it away.

We take a second step. My senses heighten. I can now hear the crunch of every awkward step we take. I can see the light wind drawing whimsical designs in the heavy falling snow. It gently whooshes past and feeds a snow bank, moving from our right to left.

*Right to left. Ugh.*

I resolve to learn cardinal directions after this trip. That is, if we survive. A loud crack of a tree branch breaking jolts us and we nearly lose our balance. I remind Melissa to breathe.

A third step.

I have now positioned myself between her and the moose. And while I want to hold Melissa's hand, I know that it would likely cause one or both us to fall. I begin to run through scenarios.

They all end in me getting crushed by the weight of a moose pressing down directly on me or onto a tennis racquet and then onto me, effectively spaghetti-fying my body. But some scenarios allow Melissa to escape. So I begin to focus on how to create the longest distraction for her.

For just a split second, I realize this is the first person I've thought about giving my life for.

It's a bad idea, but I grab Melissa's hand.

"Mel, whatever happens, you'll be okay."

She doesn't hear me. She's fumbling with her day bag and pulls out her binoculars. As I watch her peering through them, I can see tears mixing with snow, all of it melting on her face.

And, then, something strange happens. Mel starts laughing. Slowly, at first, but then so hard that she falls butt-first into the snow.

I assume she has had a mental breakdown and descended into hysteria, so I try to get her to calm down.

While she can't even breathe from the laughing, she finds a moment to say, "no, no" and hands me the binoculars.

I look through the unfocused lens, but I see it too.

The moose is a statue.

I turn the knob to get better focus.

The moose is now clearly a statue.

\* \* \*

We pass the metal protector, full of shame and joy and see our group having dinner across the windowed wall.

"Find anything out there?" says Earl, sarcastically. He has two completely overfilled buffet plates in his hands. I look at his wife Phyllis who already has her own plate. I look at all the seniors who are completely content with every aspect of this trip. And then I look at my girlfriend--now wife--who is shivering.

But she's safe.

I smile.

"Yea, Earl. Found something."

*Queenstown, New Zealand (2007)*

- Mom, say something.
- What do I say? Just wow!

# | twenty-two |

## My Heartstrings

**New Zealand, June 2007**

W e are being treated like prisoners.

Earlier in the day, they stripped us of our watches and jewelry at the processing center. And now we look the part: baggy orange jumpsuits, serious faces. Standing over that bridge, we hear the metal links click and lock into place. My mother and I look over the edge.

She grabs my sleeve. I close my eyes.

*How the hell did we get here?*

**Edison, NJ, December 2006, 6 months earlier.**

"Hey, how was lunch?" It's a pretty innocent question for a mother to ask her son. At least it's nothing to get worked up about. Yet why is my blood boiling over a simple text?

Well, for starters, I'm in my early twenties and living at home.

With my parents.

In New Jersey.

On this particular morning, mom drops me off at the Metropark train station. Before I leave the car, she runs through a list of things *I have to do,* every possible mind-numbing chore imaginable.

On the train ride into work, I get a call from dad which I let go to voicemail. Then a text from him vibrates my pants with a local news article of some murder or another he has found in New York City. He follows it with another text.

"Be safe."

"I'll try not to get murdered..." I text back, "but no promises."

That should get his heart moving.

Cracking my knuckles, I get to work. This is a big law firm in Manhattan in a piercing skyscraper with the coveted address, One New York Plaza. It's supposed to be important work. But I'm a paralegal. And all I really do is compare one spreadsheet to another. Expertly.

Day in. Day out.

I begin to fill out my billing for the week. "Billing" means taking out a couple of hours to fill out internal charts to chronicle the client charts I reviewed last week. And every action must be charted by a painstaking and specific 6 minute increment of time.

Billing forces me to think about last week not in terms of accomplishments or assignments, but as a pixelated collection of 6 minutes, perfectly arranged like sand art. Then, like a mundane mandala, I wipe it away and work on a new one the next week.

My head hurts. While most employees in other industries slow down during the holidays from the usual 40 hour work week, we've ramped up and starting calling days "Thurfri" and "Fraturday" because we were having 40 hour days.

So, I'm losing sleep, poring over the minute minutes of every 6 minutes of my time, letting chores pile up which included law school applications. Even planning our annual family Christmas party feels like tense work because of the real possibility of missing it if a surprise Fraturday rears its ugly head.

And, so, just a couple of hours into the workday, there it is.

"Hey, how was lunch?"

The text to my phone from mom.

I think about the half cut grapes my mom put into the same leftover chickpea salad she gave to my dad and me from the day before. I think of how it was something similar yesterday and would be something similar tomorrow.

But, mostly, I think about how we are all just talking for the sake of talking.

"You know how this salad is, mom." -- I text back with a period, and then lose track of time. Something has cracked.

I come home that day and tell my parents I am quitting and how I am going to travel before law school begins. I expect severe pushback, but something seemed to have stirred in mom as well.

And that's how our tradition of taking one crazy trip, just the two of us, every 5-7 years or so began.

## Back to That Bridge, New Zealand

She grabs my sleeve. I close my eyes.

*Why were we doing this again?*

We're at the Kawarau Bridge Bungee Experience. Part of what had cracked back in December was trying to get over every fear I had. And this included bungee jumping, which I'd convinced my mom would be a great idea to do together.

She is beginning to get cold feet, but ours are now literally locked together.

40 meters down, lapping around frantically, is what I assume is the Kawarau River.

"I don't think I can do this."

I look over at my mom.

*Is she trying to bail?*

"It'll be fine."

"No, Adi, I can't do this."

I freak out.

"But mom, remember the cord? We saw it at the visitor center. It's not even a cord, really. It's literally thousands of elastic bands coming together to make one strong rope, impossible to break."

She looks at me. She is not going to jump.

We were supposed to be a rope of two. I'm just a single stranded strand now. I had put all of my anxiety aside, thinking I needed to be strong for her. But now she isn't going to jump with me. They uninstall her chains and she goes to the end of the bridge where onlookers can stand and watch.

I look down. Take a deep breath. And then...

\* \* \*

I'd like to tell you this is like a movie. That when I drop, I see my childhood or something. That I see all the boring stuff and salads fly by in 6-minute increment mosaics.

But I am paralyzed and can only feel the wind whipping past my face.

On the second bounce, however, I take a long arc and can see my mom looking at me. She's just a few hundred yards away but I think I'd still see the pride beaming out even if it was miles away.

By the fourth bounce, I'm able to have coherent thoughts again. As I look at my mom, who is bouncing up and down from my frame of reference, I think about all the leaps she's already made: all her challenges stretched out of love, pulled taut through routine, and made knotted and strong through the twining of so many years. Perhaps a bungee jump does not compare to moving across worlds, making unheralded sacrifices, and dealing with a difficult son.

As I come to a stop, I'm unhooked onto a boat and I rush back to her.

She's already grabbed a bite and hands me the "free meal" that came with this expensive excursion. We get our phones back and I expect to see a bottomless string of texts from dad about bungee protocols pockmarked with "be safe."

But it just reads "Have fun" and follows with a low-resolution picture of his workday salad.

"How's the lunch?" mom asks.

It's a vegemite sandwich, objectively one of the most awful travesties ever.

And nothing's ever tasted better.

Sometimes I dream,

That he is me.

You've got to see,

That's how I dream to be.

**MICHAEL JORDAN
GATORADE COMMERCIAL (1992)**

# | twenty-three |

## My Uncle (or "The Fart Story #1")

**Chicago, Illinois (1990)**

In Indian culture, and probably a lot of other cultures, every male that is older than you is called "uncle." It's a sign of respect.

My "uncle" Sunil Nair had grown up with my dad and dad's brother in Bombay.

As a child, my dad, Dilip, often would go over Sunil's house. But not really to hang out with Sunil. Little Dilip enjoyed hanging out with Sunil's dad--who had old books and enjoyed my little dad's company while Sunil was off getting into trouble somewhere. The roots ran deep. The Nairs had already been a friend of the family for 30 years before I was even born.

This is a scenic way of saying I was supposed to call Sunil "uncle."

Yet, the first time I met Sunil, it was on a family vacation-- this time to Chicago, in 1990.

As a child, this is a typical scene. I'd get to travel a lot across the US, which is awesome.

But you should know that, in today's times, these trips would not be considered particularly Instagram-worthy. We'd get to our destination, maybe Houston or LA or Orlando or wherever, but for those 3-4 days, we were more or less in a living room. Sometimes the kitchen. And then back to a living room.

And if we're feeling really spicy, we might go back to the kitchen.

But back to Chicago. I am 6 years old and only two years in the country. Sunil and his wife are sitting on a couch in yet another living room. I am nestled in the middle of my parents on the other couch, staring into my Gameboy. Occasionally, I look up to survey my surroundings, not really making eye contact with anyone, just keeping an eye out for snacks.

No matter what city we're in, the snacks would be the

same fried chickpea batter or cornflakes or peanuts hit with spices that eventually seep deep into the skin. Today, though, it is something called nachos, from a Chi Chi's brand kit. And the TV remote, typically wrapped in plastic, is naked and sits atop a secondhand dark brown wooden coffee table. And next to it is my cold soda, without any coasters put out.

"Tell Sunil Uncle 'thank you,'" says dad as I stuff my face with nachos before anyone else did. The sides of my lips are pink, raw from being ripped apart by something called "jalapenos" and a spice level I am not used to yet. This is made worse by a Coca Cola that I think will help.

I look away from the Gameboy, roll my eyes like the little asshole I aspire to be, and say "Thank you, Sunil--" but before I can finish and call him uncle.

"Tell me something, Adi. If I asked you to fart on demand, could you do it?"

I turn off my Gameboy. Here is a man who now has my undivided attention.

"No, obviously not," I say incredulously. "That's gross," I lie.

I do not think it is gross. *What an amazing super power that would be.* But my parents are watching the interaction closely and I can feel judgment thickening the air, complicating things.

A pause cradles all of us in its arms. We look at each other not sure how to move on. But Sunil makes the slightest facial tick and then, like a large jungle cat purring, out comes the fart.

It rolls in getting heavier and more threatening. At about 6 seconds in, it peaks. Sunil's belly is undulating and creates a cacophony of sound as if a full marching band is falling over each other clumsily. 12 seconds have gone by and the smell-- old eggs and expired mango pickle--begins to blanket the whole room. I see Sunil's contorted face finally relax. A high pitched "whoop" caps off the fart, leading to a quick wince, and then a very self-satisfied smile settles in on his face.

In that exact moment, I know it. I will never call this person uncle.

And we consummate this new and uncharted type of relationship with dessert. I think it will just be some awful, soggy, cold gulab jamun, bought from the same Patel Brothers store so many other snacks are from in these elder Indian American homes. But out comes a tiny packet, a mini-dove bar. And after I ask for a second and a third, I realize there is a seemingly endless supply.

By my teenage years, I am a full-fledged Sunil fanboy, soaking in everything about his personality: his irreverence, atheism, and somewhat madcap scientific theories--e.g. perhaps we are just vehicles to keep genes alive instead of the other way around.

He is a student of history--real history--introducing me to Howard Zinn long before it is casually referenced in Good Will Hunting. We discuss some of the darker underbelly of the United States as he drives me to the United Center.

As a rabid Chicago Bulls fan who loves Michael Jordan, I am shocked to learn what life would have been like for my hero if he was born just a generation before.

Sunil often shares his deep appreciation of the Beatles and not just their songs. Rather, he can bob and weave effortlessly from speaking of their evolution, experimental drug use, place in history and also which songs helped him get laid in college.

I'd already watched Jungle Book with many family members, assuming that the thing I was supposed to enjoy was that it took place in India. But, with Sunil, all senses engage and the viewing becomes a journey of discovery into all the old and brilliant jazz standards employed in the movie. Bold and brash tunes in a style that was never before or later risked by Disney.

He is also a student and teacher of comedy. An obscure moment from the cult favorite, Half Baked, once led to literal hours dissecting a 2 minute scene.

*Villian: Where you from, from Jamaica?*

*Chappelle: Right'on the beach, boi!*

*Villian: You know what I'm gonna do? I'm going to take your little Mexican friend here. And I'm gonna kill him.*

*Cuban: Eh, yo, I'm Cuban, B!*

*Villain: Yes, Cuban B.*

"Yes, Cuban B" sends us rolling around the couch. The first Cuban B is "I'm Cuban" then a comma, then "B" -- as one might say "homie."

So, "I'm Cuban, dude," basically.

But the villain tramples over that comma and just thinks "Cuban B" is a phrase.

*Did the villain impromptu the line? Was this written in the screenplay? When the moment happens on set, does the director do several takes? Did the director even know of the genius that had just happened?*

So that would be an entire unforgettable afternoon. And those afternoons became years.

\* \* \*

Sunil passed away some time ago, in his 50s, leaving two teenagers behind that called him dad. A wife that called him husband. And my parents who called him a lifelong friend.

In the end, I'm glad I never called him uncle.

You see I think maybe "Uncle" is a spell. It can immediately erect a wall or dam of social mores and respect--which sound great--but they only allow in vapid conversations over dry, store-bought dhokla and other boring Indian snacks.

"Uncle" is a sterile plastic cover making sure the TV remote never gets any food or grubby fingerprints on it. "Uncle" would've stopped me from truly getting to know all the imperfections and stopped me from getting into the cracks of the man.

Getting into the cracks.

I feel like that matters--when you come across a lover, a father, a friend ... who can fart on call.

**You can probably find Sunil yourself...**
*hint: he's in a Beatles Let It Be T-shirt. Arms crossed like he doesn't want to be here.*

Miss you, Sunil. Hope you get to read my book somehow.

Till our genes meet again...

END OF BOOK ONE

But there's no way I'd do that thing like in the Marvel movies where there's a teaser trailer for the sequel after the credits, right?

Of course not.

That's a bit too kitschy for my tastes.

In fact, you really shouldn't look past the Author and Acknowledgments sections. ;)

Nothing to see there. Move along. Go file taxes now or whatever, loser.

# About the Author

This is Aditya Surendran's first collection of short stories.

Prior to authorship, he has played the roles of student, economist, and lawyer. He now serves in various capacities at technology startups.

He is son to his parents, Dilip and Kirti Surendran. Aditya is married to his wife, Melissa Danielson Surendran.

They live in Edison, NJ.

Of course.

# ACKNOWLEDGMENTS

A friend from college took a personal narrative writing class after we graduated. With school out of the way, her hope was to finally write her own great American novel/biography. However, the class had a reverse and chilling effect. By the end of it, she felt her stories weren't worth telling because "not enough things had happened to [her] yet."

This felt so wrong to me: that a person's stories might not be considered worthy of ink on paper, that a life could be somehow dismissible. Even 15 years later, I feel like I'm still railing against this pernicious idea; fighting back to defend the dignity of unremarkable stories. That someone might want to erase these stories is the driving force behind why I write about farts and failing to catch fish.

Even though the good money is on you probably never reading these words, AC, I hope you've found something you deem worth writing about. Better yet, I hope you realize your life has always been highly readable.

\* \* \*

I mention all this because motivation comes in myriad forms and presents a unique challenge to an Acknowledgments section. I truly believe every person I've loved, hated, looked up to, and been beaten up by that one time have all played a major role in these stories. So thank you to all of you. I hope you've gotten at least half as much value as I have out of us knowing each other.

Vinay Sanapala, thank you for nurturing my talent and convincing me that big, crazy ideas like making a book are even possible. Ayan Gupta, you've had my back since the Second Grade. I also expect you to confirm all these stories as true if it ever comes into question.

Ana-Maria Lafuente, Abbey Baker, Arshad Rahat, Bryan Bach, Carlin Moore, Damien Picault, Diem-Mi Lu, Jubin Dave, Julisa Marmolejos, Farrah Kim, Keeley Mc-Carty, Logan Crowl, Mona Sheth, Nicola Harrison, Pedro DeLancastre, Ronak Desai, Sachin Desai, Sara Chai Butler, Sean McDonald, Sonny Chatrath, Tomi Vest, and Vishal Rawal -- you've held up metaphorical giant foam fingers to cheer on all my weird ideas. Love you to the moon.

Sean Wellington, Kurt Mullen, Shymala Dason, Stephanie Rogers, Melissa Reaves, Jeff Stein, Chandreyee Lahiri, Mary Jo Pollack, Richard Munchkin, Bob Dancer, Dan Squander, Shweta Bhatt, and all the storytellers I've met during the pandemic that simply let me breathe the same air as them. I've honed these stories further down and pushed them further out with your guiding hands.

Thank you to my partners who have lent me their stages, awards, audiences, podcasts, and brands: Kevin Allison (Risk!), Carly Ann Filbin (UCB + Brash), Chris Lundy & Danielle Marino (Fringe Festival and First Person Arts); Nisse Greenberg & Erin Barker (Story Collider), Kimberly Hoyos (The Covid Story Project in partnership w/ Feeding America), Deanna Moffitt (The Antidote), and so many others. Lastly, Anna Willis Collier (PBS, Stories from the Stage), you've taught me the most important lesson of all during this journey. Thank you.

This book began as a Kickstarter--which is a synonym for a leap of faith. And so many of you took this chance without immediate gratification. To all of the co-organizers and performers of the Kickstarter events, thank you so much. The dream couldn't have become a reality without you. This includes our kickoff event performers and panelists: Pooja Khetani (poet), Sirtaj Kaur (singer), Dilip Rajan (singer), Payal Kumar (poet), Devang Doshi (producer), and our comedy headliner Sid Singh.

And my infinite thanks to those who helped support me and my mom as we tried to create a variety show/dosa making class. Though we did this all without any formal video training, we truly felt like all the talented performers caught us and turned the show into something really special. So here's to you Sabeen Sadiq (comedian), Saira Lamba Malhotra (chef), Sarah Arceo (singer), and Meghna Hegde (food blogger). Mom and I cherish you.

Some of you were seasoned performers and some of you performed your poetry, singing, or comedy for the first time. Thank you for blessing the CheeseDosa stage with your talent -- specifically at such a difficult time in our collective history.

My Subcontinental Drift family, thank you so much for making a space for South Asian nerds with a creative itch to scratch. To Payal Kumar, Adi Nochur, Salwa Tareen, Alykhan Mohamed, Bunty Singh, and Amita Vempati (Boston and DC Chapters) who have taught me that a community is something you serve, not the other way around. Neerali Patel and Dr. Faizan Syed, both of whose poetry reminds me that even if my plots are silly, my words can crack the earth, with sugar and salt.

And, of course, Tara Sarath. New York is the only city where so many can be so lonely together. Thank you for making it a little bit smaller, for pushing me further, and bringing so many together. You are sheer will sculpted into one sarcastic woman. Thank you for the tough love and the 5 minutes -- *often longer but I won't tell anyone* -- every month for so many years now.

\* \* \*

And, lastly, there's my in-laws, my parents, and Melissa. Kathi and Kim, thank you for sharing your world, your joy, your annual campsite, your bears, your vehicle with functioning door locks, your solo cups and your wait-out-the-bear wine bottles. Oh, and thank you for sharing at least a third of your most precious assets with me.

As for the rest of you three, you already got Thank-You's at the beginning of the book and, like, one section ago. But I know if I didn't put you here again, you'd be all in a tizzy about it.

Love you mom, dad, and Melissa.

Thank you for making life so fun to write about.

*Coming Soon: The Sequel to "CheeseDosa: The Book!"*

TWO CHEESE B'ADI, HEY
(A WORKING TITLE)

(TURN PAGE FOR TEASER TRAILER)

# (EXCERPT) MY FIRST KISS

**Edison, NJ (Spring 2001)**

"Mooooo!"

I stop chewing.

*Is that what I think it is?*

The sound is electronic and thin. Faint but distinct.

*She's on.*

I look at what's still left on my plate.

Some bhindi—love bhindi--so this should take maybe 2-3 seconds to clear through.

The rice is some yellowish color for presentation's sake. Mom has also laced it with raisins to impress Jagjit Uncle but this disturbing act renders the rice inedible. Thinning it all out onto the plate to appear eaten will take 30 seconds.

And as for the lentils, well ... they are sandy, will take forever to chew, and be a complete time suck.

There's no elegant solution. Just face the music—I will get in trouble for leaving the lentils.

I finish the bhindi and make a little Zen garden out of the rice. With five seconds to spare, and before Jagjit Uncle can start talking about his perfect two kids, I bolt out of my seat and crash up the stairs to my room.

"You haven't touched your daal!" Mom's voice chases me up the steps.

"Homework, mom!"

"You see how much daal I finished?" chimes in dad-- ever the Robin to her Batman--even though I'm already on a different floor of the house by now.

I throw open the door to my room, click on the giant

20-inch CRT monitor's power button, and shove aside all the homework on my desk while I wait for the screen to slowly fade in.

*10 seconds feels like an infinite wait...oh shit, my notes!*

I feel around the bottom of the bed blindly looking for my new Eastpak backpack.

*Everyone cool has a Jansport this year. How do they all just know which one to flock to? Why am I always one season behind? And how the hell did all of them get their initials on it-- with the middle one bigger than the first and last? I don't even think Kmart offers that. And when did everyone get a middle name anyway? Why didn't my parents at least give me one of those? They're free.*

With endless mini pockets and side zippers, I unzip the Eastpak's main line to the larger textbooks.

*Was it Math or Physics? Math or Physics?*

I try the physics textbook first, rifling through the second half of the book. There it is! My piece of paper titled "Talking Points." It's stuffed inside some section on light being a particle with wave properties.

I iron it out with my hand.

The computer is on now. The screen saver is a couple of jagged fractals dancing with each other--just one of the default options. I click away from it to see the home screen, briefly. My completed Solitaire game is hurling down ribbons of cards. It is unrelenting and now taking up most of the screen space.

I close out of the game and save my Catcher in the Rye essay before closing Word too. It's some piece about how Holden Caulfield is actually more of a Siddhartha Gautama/Buddha character than a Jesus figure. Mrs. Green is extremely excited about the idea, but I know I'll disappoint her with grammar issues and sentence structure.

*But we're close. My heart is beating faster now.*

Invariably, I know she'll share a song with me I've never heard before. So I should be ready to download it and pretend to know it. I open up Napster and my music player.

"Winamp! It really kicks the llama's ass!"

*That intro never gets old.*

I look through the list of blinking AOL Instant Messenger screen names and somewhere at the bottom of all of them, there she is.

My fingers move to the keyboard.

"Yo yo."

One is too casual. More than two would look desperate...

I hit enter and wait.

It feels like forever...